ULTIMATE
ONLINE COURSE CREATION
GUIDE

BY FRANK KANE

Ultimate Online Course Creation Guide
Copyright © 2018-2019 Sundog Software LLC

All rights reserved.
No part of this book may be reproduced, stored in a retrieval system,
or transmitted in any form or by any means, without the prior written permission of the publisher,
except in the case of brief quotations embedded in critical articles or reviews.

Every effort has been made in the preparation of this book to ensure the accuracy of information presented.
However, the information contained in this book is sold without warranty, either express or implied.

Neither the author, or Sundog Software, and its dealers and distributors will be held liable
for any damages caused or alleged to be caused directly or indirectly by this book.

First published: December 2018

ABOUT THE AUTHOR

Frank Kane spent nine years at Amazon and IMDb,
developing and managing the technology that automatically delivers
product and movie recommendations to hundreds of millions of customers.

Frank holds 17 issued patents in the fields of distributed computing,
data mining, and machine learning

CONTENTS BY CHAPTER

CHAPTER 1 – To Begin 1

CHAPTER 2 – How Udemy Works 11

CHAPTER 3 – Choosing Your Topic 35

CHAPTER 4 – Getting to Work 53

CHAPTER 5 – Recording Your Course 76

CHAPTER 6 – Post-Production 116

CHAPTER 7 – Udemy SEO Tips 132

CHAPTER 8 – Pre-Launch Planning 158

CHAPTER 9 – Marketing Your Course 203

CHAPTER 10 – Maintaining Your Course 225

CHAPTER 11 – Licensing Your Course 252

CHAPTER 12 – Udemy Full-Time 262

CHAPTER 13 – Wrapping Up 277

CHAPTER 1 – To Begin

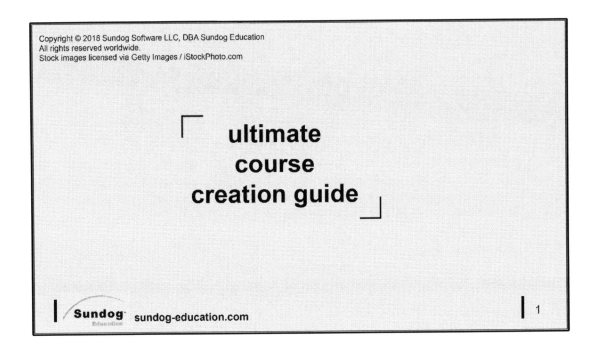

Fundamentally, this is information about making successful online courses – and this book itself should serve as a good example of one! With that in mind, I'm going to start off a little bit out of sequence, because a very important element of a successful course is what we call the "quick win."

your "quick win"

To begin, the reality is that most students won't finish your course. You can really only count on someone watching the first few minutes of it, and they might be prompted to leave a review for your course just based on those first few minutes that they saw.

The experience you deliver within the first ten minutes or so of your course is more important than anything else. You need to make sure your course is at its best during the first couple of lectures, and that you deliver some real, concrete value to the student during those first ten minutes so they feel like they got their money's worth right away. On Udemy in particular, most of your reviews are going to come from students who have only watched the first ten minutes.

This is the "quick win."

Your challenge is to deliver a sense of accomplishment to the student right away somehow. In technical courses, this might involve getting everything set up and running a simple example of whatever the student wants to learn how to build. In this book, I'm going to hit you with not one, but two "quick wins" in hopes of earning a good early review from you. The first is just telling you about "quick wins" and how important they are. I'm also going to give you one of the most important practical tips in the book right up front.

We will have a whole section on A/V gear later on, however the thing people seem to ask the most about is how to get good audio quality on their course. This is something I struggled with for over a year, and through trial and error I found that the solution is surprisingly simple.

The main problems you're likely to face are dealing with noise in your surroundings, echo from your room, and getting the right levels. And all of these problems can be solved with just positioning your microphone correctly. The idea is to pick up as much of your voice as possible, and as little of everything else. The microphone I'm using here is called a Blue Yeti, and it's a popular choice, but you'll see a lot of people disparaging it because they are frustrated in getting good results from it. Usually they'll say it's "too sensitive."

But look around me in that photo. I'm just in my office. There is no acoustical treatment here at all, and in fact I can hear a bit of an echo when I'm talking in it. I think you'll agree that my audio sounds pretty good from my microphone. It really comes down to knowing how to use it.

First of all, you want to make sure your mic is set in directional mode. On the Blue Yeti, there's a heart-shaped "cardioid" pattern on that back to select that mode. This way, it cuts out sounds from behind the mic and focuses on what's directly in front of it – which is you.

Secondly, you need to know where the "front" of the mic is. On the Blue Yeti, you don't point the mic at your mouth. You talk into the side of it, into the side that has the Blue logo on it. The gain and pattern knobs should be on the back.

Most importantly, you need to get the front of the mic in just the right place relative to your mouth. You really can't do this using the desk stand that comes with it; that's why I have a boom arm attached to my desk. This allows me to position my microphone at the same level as my mouth. The ideal position is given by the distance between your extended thumb and pinkie fingers – that's how far the mic should be from your mouth.

You also don't want to be talking directly into the microphone, or else you'll pick up a lot of "plosives." That's a popping sound that happens when you say letters like P directly into the mic. You'll also pick up a lot of your breathing if you're aiming your mouth directly at the mic. You can buy "pop filters" which help a little, though an even more effective solution is to just position the microphone a little bit off to the side, still pointing toward your mouth. That way, your breath flows past the mic instead of directly into it, but the mic is still at the right distance and orientation to pick your voice loudly and clearly.

You'll also notice I also have a shock mount attached to the mic, which then attaches to the boom arm. This helps me to avoid noise if I bump the table, or even just from typing on it.

Finally, you need to find the right setting for your gain knob through trial and error. Mine's set about ¼ of the way up, but the right setting for you will depend on how loudly you speak. You need to set it so that it fills up the waveform in your video editor while you're talking at your loudest, without clipping the peaks of those waves.

To recap – good audio quality is mostly about good microphone placement. Make sure you're talking into the front of the microphone, and it's not always obvious where that is. Make sure your mic is directional. Make sure it's at the same level as your mouth, a bit off to the side, pointing toward you, and a thumb-and-pinky away. You'll probably need a boom arm to do this, and a shock mount is worth the extra investment.

So, there's your "quick win!" And again, your courses also need to have a "quick win" because students are going to evaluate you and your course very early on. You need to deliver real, concrete value in those first few minutes in order for those crucial first reviews to be positive ones.

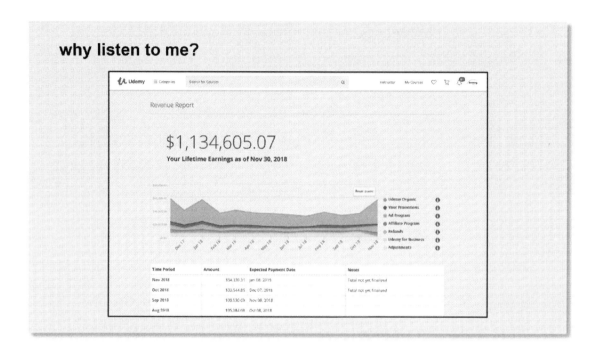

There are a *lot* of books and courses like this, so let's get the question of *"why you should listen to me"* out of the way first.

Well, whatever I'm doing has worked. This is my revenue chart on Udemy showing my monthly income since I started in the fall of 2015. Over three years, I've earned over one million dollars just from Udemy. This chart is the money that's actually deposited into my bank account; it's not the gross sales of my courses – it's the net amount I earned as an individual, after splitting the revenue with everyone else who gets a cut of it. And this is just from Udemy – I also sell my courses on other platforms that bring in even more revenue, although Udemy is by far the largest source.

Today I'm consistently earning around $30,000 per month just from Udemy, and as you can imagine that is a life-changing sort of thing. I just make courses for a living from the comfort of my own home now.

I don't deal with a daily commute, endless meetings and office politics, or a strict nine-to-five schedule. I can work when I want to, wherever I want to, however I want to. And I don't really worry about money as much anymore. If I want to travel someplace or do something with my family, I don't have to beg my boss to allow me the time off and worry about how I'll pay for it – I pretty much just do it.

I don't mean to brag; I just want you to understand that the tips I'm going to give you have the potential to change your life too. You should pay attention. I certainly can't promise that you'll make a million dollars if you do everything I say in this book, because a lot of it does come down to luck, timing, the amount of work you're able to put into it, and the topics you're able to teach. I'm going to tell you everything I've done in order to get to this point, and you don't have to learn it all the hard way like I did.

My goal is to maximize your odds for success as an online instructor, by sharing proven techniques with you.

実践データサイエンス&機械学習 with Python -統計学の基礎からビッグデー... 米露 LIVE ¥15,000 - Public	Earned This Month $251.67 Total Earned $5,774.57	Course Rating 3.80	Enrolled This Month 210 Total students 3,987	Unanswered Questions 4
The Ultimate Hands-On Hadoop - Tame your Big Data! Sundog Education LIVE $179.99 - Public	Earned This Month $14,216.76 Total Earned $257,447.38	Course Rating 4.52	Enrolled This Month 4,704 Total students 59,518	Unanswered Questions 4
Apache Spark 2 with Scala - Hands On with Big Data! Sundog Education LIVE $99.99 - Public	Earned This Month $5,535.53 Total Earned $132,622.23	Course Rating 4.48	Enrolled This Month 1,935 Total students 29,947	Unanswered Questions 0
Data Science & Maschinelles Lernen in Python - am Beispiel Jannis LIVE €124.99 - Public	Earned This Month $146.43 Total Earned $4,893.86	Course Rating 4.32	Enrolled This Month 208 Total students 5,162	Unanswered Questions 1
Taming Big Data with Spark Streaming and Scala - Hands On! Sundog Education LIVE $99.99 - Public	Earned This Month $1,429.98 Total Earned $60,386.64	Course Rating 4.42	Enrolled This Month 562 Total students 11,493	Unanswered Questions 0
Data Science, Deep Learning and Machine Learning with Python Sundog Education LIVE $159.99 - Public	Earned This Month $20,983.17 Total Earned $357,647.85	Course Rating 4.56	Enrolled This Month 6,670 Total students 77,136	Unanswered Questions 7

My techniques don't require you to produce a course every week, or even every month, either. Over three years, I've really only produced 10 courses – and two of those were co-produced with someone else, which cut my own work in half. Here you can see some of the revenue totals from my individual courses.

You can see that it's very much hit-driven; there's a very wide range in how well each course does. It makes sense to focus your efforts into creating a small number of really awesome, comprehensive courses that are positioned to become best-sellers, instead of just shoveling out as many courses as you can. I'm going to show you how to do that.

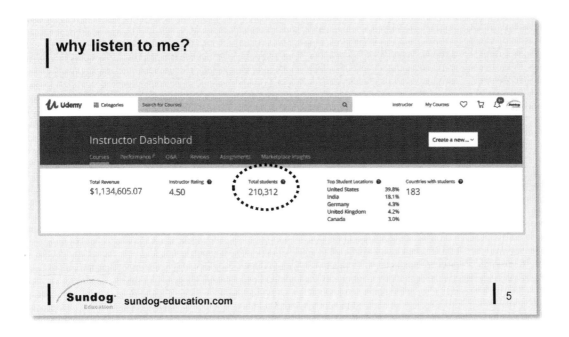

I want to also stress that this isn't all about the money, either. It's about the impact. Money in itself isn't a very fulfilling thing, and focusing on money alone can lead to a lot of stress and disappointment as that revenue fluctuates over time. The real power of Udemy is its reach; it offers an opportunity to share your knowledge with millions of people all over the world. I've reached well over 200,000 students who have paid real money to take my online courses.

Every week, I hear from students who landed a better job or an entirely new career that started with what I taught them. Udemy offers you a chance to change the lives of people on a global scale, at prices that are accessible to anyone.

I've even randomly bumped into my students on the street on a few occasions. Udemy's platform is a really amazing opportunity to measurably change the world, improve the lives of others, and spread knowledge – all while making a good living for yourself at the same time. I want to teach you how to expand your own impact on the world in the same way I did.

That's part of why I'm making this book in the first place – if you can achieve the same success that I did, then together we'll double the impact I've already made.

CHAPTER 2 – How Udemy Works

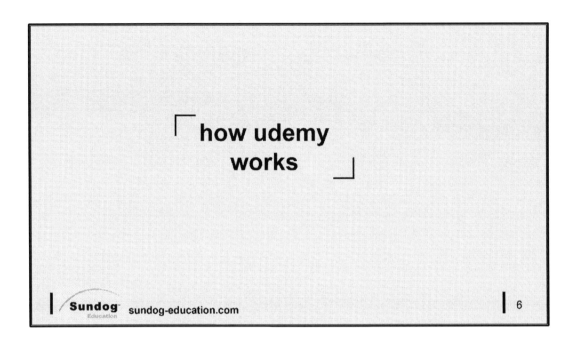

When I first got started with Udemy, I had a lot of misconceptions about how it worked and what would be expected from me in the long term. If you're an experienced instructor, you can probably skip this section - however if you're new to Udemy, there are a few things you need to understand about how the marketplace works. You don't want them to hit you as an unpleasant surprise; it's better to know about them up front, so you can plan accordingly.

When I first started on Udemy, my biggest misconception was about the prices students actually pay for courses. When I was considering making my first Udemy course, I saw all of these courses on the platform that appeared to have thousands of students, with a list price of hundreds of dollars. It looked like almost everyone was making hundreds of thousands of dollars from every individual course!

As it turns out, that's not the case at all. Udemy students have come to expect steep discounts on courses, and to only actually pay $10 - $15 for a course even if its list price is in the hundreds.

On the rare occasions that a student purchases a course at list price, it's usually followed up by a refund once that student realizes they could have had it much more cheaply if they just waited for the next sale – and there's always a sale going on.

Your initial reaction may be that you're insulted by people only valuing your course creation at $10, but you're going to have to get over it. You're competing with platforms like YouTube, where people can learn things for free, or with books, which don't sell for much more than that either. And you're also selling your course in markets that are very price-conscious, where even $10 might be a stretch for many people. That's just how it goes, and the sooner you come to terms with that, the better.

It gets worse – you don't even get that full $10. On average, you'll only actually receive around $4 per course enrollment once everyone else takes their share.

Oh, and you can't really tell how many students actually bought a given course on Udemy, either. Many instructors inflate their enrollment numbers by offering lots of free coupons, or even offering their course for free for a while. I don't recommend doing that, and we'll talk more about pricing strategies later on.

You really can't use the number of students enrolled in a course as a signal as to how many students are actually engaged with that course, or how many students have actually paid for it.

The reality is that your course will only sell at a very low price point on Udemy, and the growth of your student base will be slow at first. It's best to understand that up front, so you aren't disappointed when your first course starts off slow. Everyone's first course starts off slow, no matter how good it is. With some persistent effort, you can build it up into something big.

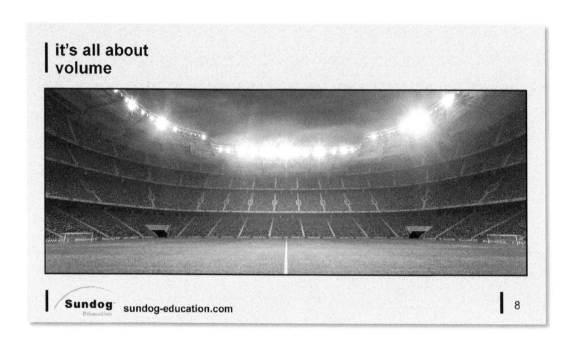

So how do you earn a living selling courses when you only get around $5 for every person who enrolls? It's all about the volume. Volume is what Udemy offers you – the ability to sell your course in front of millions of people who are actively seeking knowledge. Your focus needs to be on the reach your course is having, not how much each student is paying. It's the product of students and price that leads to your own bottom line, so even if the price is small, a really large student base still produces a large number.

In my case, 200,000 students have purchased my courses, and on average I received $5 from each of them. That works out to a million dollars.

That sort of reach is not typical; most instructors don't come close to that, to be honest. But it's also not all that exceptional; I've met many instructors who put me to shame.

Again, this isn't something to get upset about. Udemy is constantly running experiments to find the optimal price points for courses, and they are trying to maximize overall revenue for both them and for us. They arrived at a $10 price point because they know that drives the optimal number of sales, and they'll continue to adjust price points to maximize total revenue across different markets.

Rather, you should be excited about the impact on the world this enables for you as an instructor. I put up a picture of a filled football stadium to help you envision the reach that Udemy makes possible. The largest football stadiums hold around 100,000 people. If I were to teach my course live to everyone who has enrolled in it on Udemy, I'd be teaching to a sold-out stadium like that – and I'd have to do it twice, and maybe even three times, because they all wouldn't fit in there. You're reading this to hopefully enable yourself to achieve that sort of reach too.

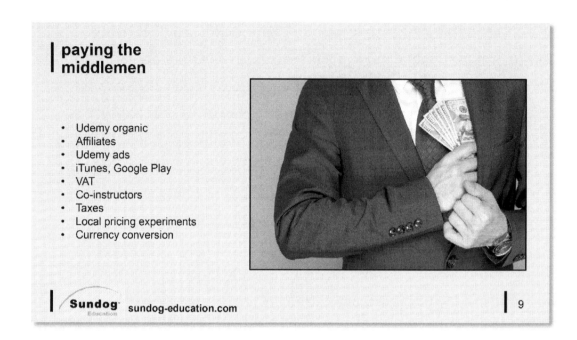

Another thing that new Udemy instructors are unpleasantly surprised by is how many other people end up taking a cut of their course revenue. Spare yourself some pain, and take time to understand how it all works up front. The only case in which you get most of that $10 a student spends is when you have referred that student to Udemy yourself using your own promotional coupon code, and an affiliate hasn't already tagged that student. In that case, you get 97% of the revenue – the remaining 3% goes toward covering credit card processing fees and things like that.

So, no matter what, the banks that handle these transactions between Udemy and its students are taking a small cut.

The whole reason you're on Udemy is to get exposure to the students on their marketplace. And if a student discovers your course by browsing or searching on the Udemy platform, Udemy takes 50% of that sale as a commission. That's the deal. But these are sales you would not have been able to make on your own, so it's all basically free money to you. And you'll find that this traffic, which is called "Udemy organic" traffic, will make up the bulk of your actual revenue. These are enrollments where Udemy did all of the marketing for you. You did not do the work of finding those students, they did.

Another source of enrollments is from affiliates. These are external websites that refer traffic to Udemy and market courses on their behalf to a wider audience. If a student comes to Udemy from an affiliate site, that student is tagged with a browser cookie that will credit that affiliate with anything they buy in the coming 7 days. That affiliate tag supersedes everything else, so even if you bring a student to Udemy using your own promotional coupon code, the affiliate will still get credit for that sale if they got to them before you did. For affiliate sales, you only receive 25% of the resulting revenue. This stings a lot, and yes there are cases where an affiliate can seem to "steal" a sale that you drove yourself.

On the whole, they are delivering new students to Udemy and to your courses that you would not have had otherwise. The 25% you receive may sting, but it's still more than nothing. And all you're selling is digital assets – there's really nothing for you to lose from it.

You also only receive 25% of a sale when it comes from online ads that Udemy ran on your behalf. If Udemy sees that your course is converting well, they may start to purchase ads for it on your behalf – and of course, they need to cover the costs of those ads. It's really very reasonable that you receive a lower portion of what the student paid in this case. Typically, this isn't a big part of your revenue, anyhow, as Udemy uses ads sparingly, and the effectiveness of online ads in general seems to be declining over time.

Another culprit is mobile app platforms such as the iTunes store and Google Play. Any app that makes sales on these platforms is required to give 30% of their revenue to the platform. It sounds ridiculous, and kind of is, that's just how it works – not just for Udemy, but for anyone selling things on apps sold through these stores. Any time someone buys your course through Udemy's mobile app, the app store it came through gets a 30% cut of the revenue before everyone else, including Udemy, gets their share. In that case, you'll typically get 50% of the remaining 70% of the sale price, since that's a "Udemy Organic" sale.

Udemy is also required to collect value-added tax, or VAT, from students in Europe. This also gets subtracted from the sale price before things get divided up further.

If you've teamed up with any co-instructors, including teaching assistants, who you've set up to be paid on a revenue share basis, you'll also have to share any earnings with them as well.

You shouldn't be surprised by deals like this that you made yourself, but you might be surprised when only receive one dollar from a given sale because only two dollars was left over after everyone else took their cuts, and you had to split that two dollars with someone else.

Remember you're going to be responsible for any taxes on the income you receive from Udemy, too. This is taxable income. If you just spend all the money you receive from Udemy, you're going to find yourself with a very painful tax bill the following year if you didn't set aside enough to cover those taxes.

Udemy also conducts pricing experiments in different countries, so there are situations where courses may be offered below $10. Again, they're just trying to find the optimal price point in each region that leads to the most overall revenue, so they're doing this in your best interests.

Finally, currency conversion rates can take a big bite out of your earnings too. If you're selling courses in a country whose currency has been de-valued, such as Turkey, you end up losing a lot of that sale amount once it's converted into your local currency.

I'm not trying to be a downer here, I just want to make sure you're not surprised by any of this when you see it happening for the first time. This is how Udemy works. And again, even though you may only make a few dollars per course enrollment, Udemy's large student base means you can make up for that with volume, if you're teaching a topic that is in high demand.

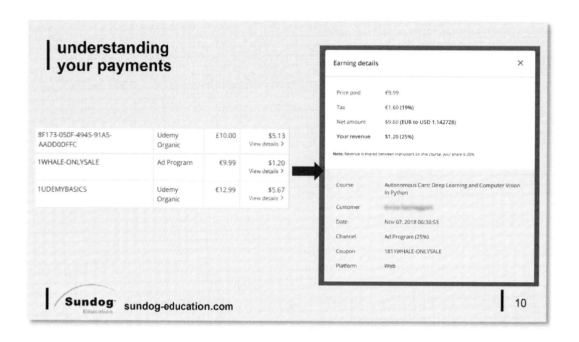

Let's go over a real example from my own revenue report. If you click on a month in your revenue report in Udemy's instructor dashboard, you'll see a listing of every sale your course has made.

So, I might wonder why I only made $1.20 on this particular course sale. Udemy is totally transparent with this; just click on the "view details" link and they'll show you exactly how everything was carved up. In this case, it was a European student where Udemy was required to collect value-added tax of 19% on 9.99 Euros they paid, which took 1.6 Euros off the sale price right off the top. Currency conversion actually worked in our favor, though, and we got back up to $9.60 as a starting point after converting the remaining Euros into US dollars.

Things get a little confusing at this point, however. The "share" they display here is 25%, but that's based on a Udemy organic sale. On an organic sale, 50% goes to Udemy, and the remaining 50% is divided between the co-instructors of the course. In this particular course, I have a 50/50 split of revenue with the co-instructor I worked with, which means my remaining "share" is 25%. Let's see, 25% of $9.60 is $2.40 – so why did I only get $1.20?

Well, it's because this is not an organic sale, it's a sale that was driven by an ad. And Udemy needs to recover the cost of that ad, which means they get 75% of what's left over, and only the remaining 25% gets split between the co-instructors. With that in mind, the math works out – 25% of $9.60 is $2.40, and after splitting that with my co-instructor, it only leaves $1.20 for me.

This is sort of an extreme example, but again it's worth knowing that things like this happen, and there's no point getting upset about it. That's still $1.20 I wouldn't have had otherwise, and I didn't do any work to drive that sale myself. Again – it's all about volume, not how much money you get from each individual sale.

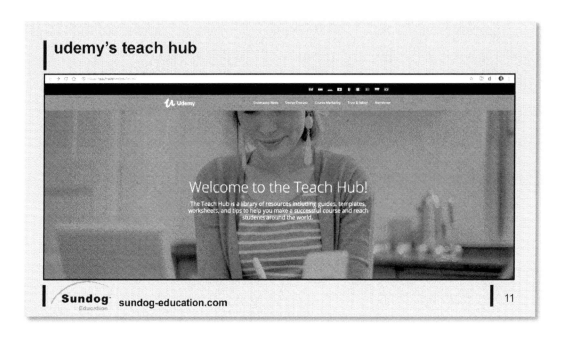

Remember, any time you have questions about how Udemy works, the mechanics of creating your course, or what Udemy's policies are, you'll find lots of awesome resources at Udemy's "Teach Hub" at teach.udemy.com. They also have some great course marketing tips there for you to look through. This book is meant to be a supplement to the materials at the Teach Hub, not a replacement for it. For simple things like "how do I upload a video into my course" or "what format should my video be in," you should be looking to the Teach Hub for answers.

I want to focus our time in this book on the tips and secrets to success that the Teach Hub doesn't cover. If you're a new instructor, you really need to read through everything on the Teach Hub before you start producing content, as it covers all the basics you need to know.

A lot of new instructors get confused about "Udemy for Business" when they first hear about it, or when they first start seeing students enroll from it.

Let's first talk about what Udemy for Business, or UFB, is. It is a subscription-based service that Udemy sells to corporations. It offers a curated selection of Udemy's best courses to those corporate clients, who are able to watch as much of them as they want for a fixed monthly fee.

Your new course will not be offered to UFB students until it meets certain standards and has proven itself in the marketplace as a quality course. They don't say exactly how they decide which courses become part of the UFB offering, but if your course gets added, you'll start to see some extra revenue added into your monthly earnings from UFB toward the beginning of each month.

As new students enroll in your course from UFB, you don't receive any money for that enrollment. You do receive a share of the total revenue UFB collects from its clients, based on how many minutes of your content was viewed by UFB students that month.

At a high level, UFB sets aside 25% of the revenue it receives from its corporate clients, and divides that 25% up amongst instructors based on how many minutes of content were viewed from each instructor's content. UFB can end up being a significant portion of your revenue once you're part of it. For me it makes up about 20% of my overall revenue from Udemy, and it's growing steadily.

The only thing you need to do to participate in UFB is make sure you're opted in to it – and we'll cover how to do that in a moment – and make courses that are good enough to be included in the program. I've heard that they try not to offer too many courses in the same topic, so if your topic is highly competitive that may make it more difficult to get included.

If you've released a new course that you believe is of high interest to Udemy's corporate clients, you can also send a quick note to ufbcontent@udemy.com to make sure they consider it for inclusion. Don't contact them until your course already has enough reviews to prove that it's of high quality. Generally speaking, if they want your course, they'll add it without you having to do anything.

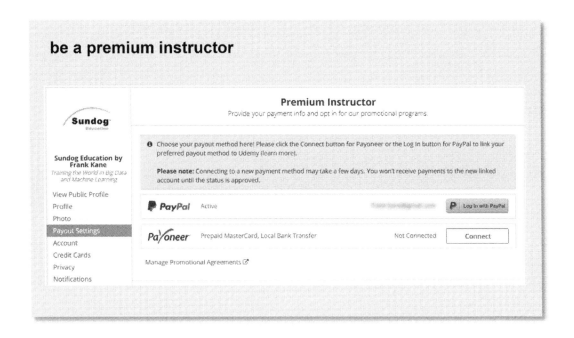

Many questions I see from new instructors also revolve around how to set things up to get paid by Udemy. In order to offer a course on Udemy for sale and not just for free, you have to set yourself up as a "premium instructor." There's no cost involved in this to you, nor is there any sort of vetting process you have to go through. A "premium instructor" is simply an instructor who has connected their Udemy account to PayPal or Payoneer so Udemy has a means of paying you for your courses.

If you don't have a PayPal or Payoneer account, you can't sell courses on Udemy. So be sure to get one. You'll find your "premium instructor" settings under the payout settings in your Udemy account. Be sure to set this up before publishing your first course. I've heard that certain tax forms may be required by Payoneer in certain countries before they'll move forward, so it's best to sort all of that out sooner rather than later if it applies to you.

Also remember you're entirely responsible for any local taxes on the money you receive from Udemy. Udemy will not withhold taxes for you, and in the US, they don't even report your income to the IRS. If you start to earn any significant amount of revenue from Udemy, you'll want to talk to an accountant to make sure you don't end up on the wrong side of the law.

Take note of the "Manage Promotional Agreements" link at the bottom of your Payout Settings screen. There are some really important things in there, which I'll cover next.

you should opt in

☑ I have read and agree to the Udemy Deals Program Terms & Conditions with the following permissions:
☑ Percentage Promotions   ☑ Fixed-Price Promotions

☑ I have read and agree to the Udemy Marketing Boost Program Terms & Conditions.

☑ I have read the Udemy For Business Content Subscription Program Terms & Conditions and elect to participate.

I advise opting into all of Udemy's promotional agreements. Udemy, as I said, is a marketplace where you sell lots of courses at a low price. If you try to sell courses at full price and don't allow Udemy to discount them, you're not going to sell any courses. Well, in principle you could do all of your own marketing and send your students to Udemy as a hosting platform – but those students are going to be upset when they see all the courses competing with yours that they could have had for $10 on Udemy.

I just don't see any scenario where opting out of Udemy's marketing makes sense. If you really just can't stand the idea of selling your course for $10, then sell it yourself on your own website. Udemy isn't adding any value if you're trying to sell courses at their list price. What Udemy offers you is volume and a large audience. You'll find it's much harder than you might think to sell your own course entirely on your own unless you're already famous and have a huge following.

There are three agreements on the "manage promotional agreements" screen you can read through an optionally opt in to. The first is for the "Udemy Deals" program. This is what allows Udemy to offer your course at a discount, either as a percentage-based discount (like "90% off all courses!") or a fixed price discount (like "Every course for $9.99!") Fixed-price promotions seem to be more common, however I see no reason to opt out of one but not the other.

Don't think that you can outsmart Udemy students by offering your course at a high list price and only opting into percentage promotions to keep your price higher. Udemy students expect fixed-price promotions at a low price, and they will pass by your course if it's not part of them. Udemy is a competitive marketplace, and if they can't buy your course for $9.99, they'll buy someone else's course instead.

The second agreement is for the "Udemy Marketing Boost" program. This is what allows Udemy to sell your course through ads or affiliates, where you only receive 25% of whatever revenue is left over. Although the role of affiliates is sometimes a touchy subject, on the whole I've found that both ads and affiliates are bringing students to you that you would not have had otherwise, so this is basically free money.

You can't opt into just one or the other, you need to accept revenue from ads and affiliates both, or it's nothing at all. I advise opting into the marketing boost program.

Finally, there is the option to be considered for Udemy for Business. Again, this is basically free money. The only downside to UFB is that their students can sometimes be a little more critical and have higher expectations of your course, and this may be reflected in the reviews they leave. In my case, 20% of my revenue wouldn't exist without UFB, and it seems like crazy talk to even think about opting out of it.

It's important to stress that Udemy is not a get-rich-quick scheme. During my first few months on the Udemy platform, I only made a few hundred dollars. The only reason I'm able to earn a living on Udemy today is because I didn't give up; I put in even more hard work to create more and more courses that I kept marketing to the people who enrolled in my earlier courses. I kept building upon that small audience I started with, until I worked it up from a trickle to a firehose of new students. Yes, I've made a million dollars from Udemy – but it's been over the span of three years, and it's really only in the past year that I could have lived off Udemy income exclusively.

In truth, I'd have more money in the bank today had I stayed in my corporate job instead – though the freedom and impact Udemy offers makes it all worthwhile.

It's very discouraging to see people who seem to be desperate for money coming onto the Udemy platform as new instructors, hoping to get rich selling courses. It just doesn't work that way. If you're having trouble paying your bills, you're not going to build up enough revenue from Udemy in your first month to do that, no matter how good you are.

Producing a course good enough to be successful often takes several months to begin with. If you're in a situation like that, you'd be much better served spending that time looking for a job or freelance work that can provide immediate income to you. Success on Udemy requires sustained effort over a period of years, and it's not something you should be doing full-time at first.

We'll talk more about how to transition into the world of self-employment with Udemy in a responsible manner toward the end of the book. You need to go into this understanding that success will not come quickly, and even when it does come, you will still need to work hard to sustain that success.

People sometimes refer to Udemy as "passive income," but it really isn't. It requires ongoing work, or you'll soon see your courses being displaced by competing ones. Devoting a steady, consistent effort toward Udemy is what leads to success in the long term.

Honestly there is no guarantee that your persistent hard work will pay off as much as you would like. At some point, you're going to have to ask yourself if it's a worthwhile effort for you. I'd like to think that my success on the platform was mostly due to hard work, however in all honesty, a lot of it was just luck.

I was lucky to be born with a voice that people seem to like listening to. So much so that they were willing to overlook some of the early mistakes I made on the A/V side with my first courses, and buy more of my courses anyhow.

I was lucky to have found myself in a long career at Amazon.com where I ended up learning highly valuable technical skills that are in high demand today. As we'll explore shortly, the topics you're able to teach are a huge factor in how well your courses will do. Plus, that experience at Amazon lent authority to me as an instructor that other people didn't have.

I was also lucky to stumble my way onto the Udemy platform 3 years ago, when it was a less competitive marketplace and many of those high-demand topics had very few courses available for them. Finding topics that are in high demand and yet underserved is a lot harder today.

I'm lucky to live in a relatively quiet suburb, where finding a quiet environment to record my courses in isn't an issue.

I hate to say it, but I was also lucky to be born as a white, American male who looks younger than he really is. We must acknowledge that many Udemy students have racial and cultural biases that apply when they're looking at which course to buy, and who they want to spend hours listening to.

Angela Yu might be held up as counter-example, being a woman of Asian descent who is several times more successful on the platform than I am. She deserves every bit of that success; I've met her and she's an amazing person. She too was lucky to have a nice voice, along with a cool British accent, and a youthful, attractive appearance. Not all instructors have those sorts of advantages before they even start.

Udemy's students are still mostly in the United States, and if you have a thick accent that's difficult for American ears, you're going to be limited in the audience you can reach.

So, I'll say it again – I'm going to give you tips to maximize your success, but I can only give you tips on the things that you can control. Not everyone can make a million dollars on Udemy. I'm here to help maximize your odds and give you some important key information about this type of business, but some things are outside of our control. That's just reality unfortunately. You won't know unless you give it a go however, so let's dig in!

CHAPTER 3 – Choosing Your Topic

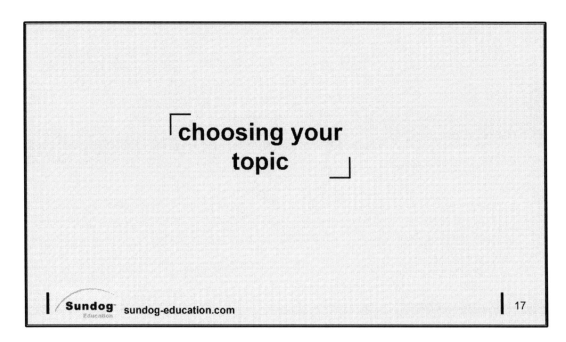

If there's one key to success, it's in choosing the right topic for your course. As we said, Udemy is a volume game, and if there isn't a large audience desperately searching for the knowledge you can provide within Udemy's student base, even the best-produced course in the world will not achieve financial success.

Let's talk about how to identify topics that are the intersection of what's in demand, and what you know about.

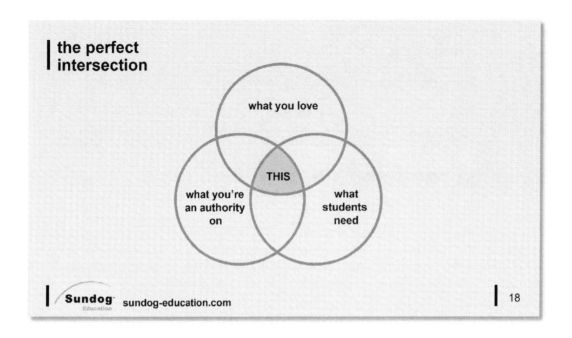

The biggest decision you can make when launching a new course is what topic you're going to teach. If you choose the wrong topic, it doesn't matter how good your course is. Teaching a topic that's not in demand, or teaching that topic poorly, will ultimately be a waste of your time. This is the one thing that is absolutely essential to figure out.

Ideally, you want to find a topic that you love and have a real interest in. That will help keep you motivated through the long process of creating a quality course in it, and make it easier to maintain your energy and enthusiasm while you're recording the course. When you're teaching something that excites you, that excitement becomes contagious to your students. That alone can set your course apart, and increase the impact it has on the people who watch it.

Think about the great teachers you had in your life – they're the ones who inspired passion in you for a given topic, and I bet they did that by demonstrating their own passion for it. If there's one guy who changed my life, it was my math teacher in high school, Mr. Foresta. He somehow made calculus fun, because he had fun with it himself while teaching it. Be like Mr. Foresta. Be a teacher who inspires, by teaching something you love.

Passion alone isn't enough, however. You have to know what you're talking about, and your potential students need to trust that you are an expert in what's being taught. Udemy does not vet its instructors in any way, nor are our courses accredited in any way.

The onus is on the student to decide whether or not you're going to teach them accurate and complete information, and not just making stuff up. You have to be able to establish yourself as an authority in your topic before students will trust you enough to teach them on it. Perhaps you can convey that authority through your professional experience, through higher degrees you've attained from college, or by running a successful business related to the topic you're teaching. You can't just go read a book and declare yourself an expert on something, and expect students to hand you money to learn from you.

You need to have some sort of real experience in the field you are teaching. Not only does it give students confidence when enrolling in your course, that experience also gives you confidence while you're teaching. Students will sense your uncertainty if you're teaching something you don't really know about, and that only leads to fewer sales and poor reviews.

The most important circle in that Venn diagram is "what students need." You already know what topics interest you, and what you're an authority on. Udemy's students couldn't care less about your personal interests. They are looking for specific skills that they need, often to improve their career, make more money, or solve some real pressing problem they are facing.

Too many instructors focus on the intersection of "what you love" and "what you're an authority on" and produce a course in that, in the name of "following their passion." If your passion is underwater basket-weaving, well, good for you – but you're not going to find anyone willing to pay even $10 on Udemy to learn underwater basket-weaving. They can learn things like that for free on YouTube, and since learning to weave baskets underwater isn't going to make money for them or further their careers, they're not going to come to Udemy actively searching for courses on that topic to spend their money on.

If you're looking for financial success on Udemy or to have any significant reach, you need to teach things that solve a real pain point for students on the Udemy platform. Things that are so painful that they are going to actively search for that topic on Udemy, and spend their money to learn about it. For example, I teach topics related to machine learning, big data, and artificial intelligence. There are a lot of people who know their technical careers can't move forward without understanding these emerging fields, and they're fearful for their livelihood if they don't learn them. What I'm selling is some confidence in emerging technology topics that will enable people to keep pushing their own technical careers forward.

It is an absolute no-brainer to spend $10 for that. Will the value of what you are teaching result in such a massive return for the student that they'll be willing to part with their money to learn it? If not, then you're not teaching the right topic.

"Need" also implies that there aren't already a bunch of awesome courses in your topic that fulfill that need. Demand for a topic is only half of the equation; you also need to make sure you can produce a course that's substantially better than the courses that already exist for that topic, if there are any.

If your competing courses already fulfill the needs these students have, what can you offer that's better? Fortunately, you don't have to guess what pain points Udemy students are struggling to solve – Udemy provides some tools for you to research this on your own. Let's cover that next.

marketplace insights

Under your instructor dashboard, you'll find a link to "Marketplace Insights," and this contains a treasure trove of data that can help you decide which topic you want to teach is most likely to succeed. It not only gives you a picture of the current student demand for your topic, it also gives you comprehensive information about the existing courses in that topic that you need to compete with.

Unless your goal is only to share information and not to reach a large audience, it would be silly not to do some research here before you start producing a course for a given topic. You may find that a slightly different topic, or more specific one, would be a much better choice – while still being able to teach something you love, and something you're an authority in.

The screen you start with contains a search bar so you can look for your topic, along with some suggestions for topics that are both in high demand and don't have many existing courses in them yet. You can see that the best topics tend to be technical in nature, with Oracle, web services, and data cleaning making the list today.

There's also a financial topic: derivatives trading. Again, these hot topics are ones that promise concrete value to the student if they can learn the information being offered – whether it's a lucrative technical career, or making money on the financial markets.

Then we have "League of Legends" – apparently a lot of people are searching for that on Udemy, though no courses currently exist for it. That one's a puzzler – why would people be looking for courses on a video game?

Well, it turns out that it's a game that's popular in "e-sports," so there are a lot of people dreaming about winning real money by playing this game in tournaments, and want an edge in their technique. If you've won a League of Legends tournament, you could probably make some extra money by making a course about it on Udemy!

Let's see if making this project, which you're now reading, was a good idea or not. I'll enter "Online Course Creation" for the topic, and select it.

You can see you can also select a language for your course, to narrow your analysis down to specific language markets. Often, a topic that is saturated in English still has a lot of opportunity in other languages. But English is the only language I speak fluently, so I'll stick with that.

According to Marketplace Insights, I should "Bring my A-game to succeed in this topic." That means that although there's a fairly high demand for courses in this topic, there's also a lot of great courses already in it. It would take a truly exceptional course to become a best-seller in this topic area.

It also gives us an idea of what success in this topic looks like – apparently the best-selling course in this area is bringing in a bit over $1,000 per month. Frankly, that's not that great – but I'd certainly welcome that sort of extra income. The median revenue however is only $16 per month! So, a course on online course creation that is just average in quality will almost certainly end up as a waste of time. That's why you need to "bring your A-game to succeed."

Don't stop here – there's even more data to look at!

The "search volume percentile across topics" is a very quick way to see how much demand there really is for this topic. The truly huge opportunities that are bringing in six figures per month for top instructors are in the 99th percentile. The value of topics drops off very quickly once you get below 99%, so if you're truly aiming to live like millionaire, you need to be teaching topics in that 99th percentile, and crushing the competition in that category somehow.

Online course creation ends up in the 93rd percentile, which may sound good, but it really isn't that great because the truly awesome opportunities are up at 99%. This tells me that even if I end up crushing it in this topic, it's not going to generate the sort of money that will allow me to go live on an island for the rest of my life and never work again.

Realistically, it could help to maintain my existing revenue stream from Udemy and maybe pay for a few more nights out with my family. Given the amount of work I expect the creation of the course to involve, it seems like a pretty good bet to me so far.

You can see the trends in search volume for this topic over the past several months. It's basically holding steady, from the looks of things. I'd rather pick a topic that's increasing in popularity, but at least it's not really decreasing in any significant way either.

You can also see the top search keywords for your topic here. Write these down for your topic! These are the keywords you want to focus on for SEO purposes later on. When someone types "Udemy" in the search bar, I want to make sure my course comes up in the list. And that means I need to use the word "Udemy" a lot on my course landing page, as well as the phrase "online course."

If you've gotten to this point and concluded that there probably isn't a big enough opportunity to warrant the time you'd put into making your course, there's a list of similar topics that you might want to explore instead. This is really helpful in guiding you toward the best topic to teach, given your broader area of expertise that you started your search with. Really, the people at Udemy who designed this did an awesome job.

But wait, there's more! If we look further, we'll actually see what the top existing courses in this topic are, so we can see how hard it will be to compete with them.

Here, you can see what it is you're up against. Keep in mind that many students buy more than one course on the same topic, so it's not really a winner-takes-all sort of situation. It's good to know what exactly is meant by "bringing your A-game". Specifically, you need to at least be as good as the top courses that exist in this category, and here they are for you to explore.

Unsurprisingly, Phil Ebiner's course is at the top. He's a great guy, makes great courses, and has achieved similar success to my own, and I highly recommend that you take his course too. If I were out to take over this category however, I'd have to offer something substantially better than what he's offering – so much better that students would enroll in my new course instead of his well-established, highly rated one. That's kind of a tall order.

As I look at the top courses in this category, a couple of things stick out to me. First, none of them are longer than 8 hours, and the top-selling course is only 5 ½ hours long. That's an achievable length to meet or exceed. Since students are usually buying courses on fixed price promotions, they will tend to go for courses that have more content in them given the choice, since for them they all cost the same price regardless of length. Students want to get the most value for their money, even when it's only $10. So, if I really wanted to dominate this category, I'd produce a 10-hour or longer course to do so.

That's not really my goal, so this course is only going to be as long as it needs to be. It seems that the "table stakes" for this category is a course that's around 5 hours in length. Good to know.

Also, as I dig into these courses, none of them have been updated recently. So that's another opportunity for my course to stand out – I'm offering the latest information, taking all of the changes that have happened on Udemy in the past year into account. And it has in fact changed quite a bit during that time.

However, the top courses in this category are very highly rated, so students are going to have very high-quality expectations from any new course in this category. If I were seeing lower ratings on the existing courses, then I might feel more optimistic because I'd know I could beat them on review scores, which would give my new course a big advantage. Phil's score, however, is really hard to beat – so I'm not going to win just on quality alone.

What's our final conclusion about choosing online course creation for our topic?

I should set my expectations at a few hundred dollars of revenue per month it seems, but "bringing my A-game" to compete among the existing courses in this category does in fact seem achievable. I guess I'll keep recording and set my sights high!

As a different example, let's say I were thinking about creating a course in web development. This also comes up as an area of high demand, but with high competition. Sometimes that can be OK if you think you can do a much better job than the existing top-sellers in the topic. Web development is so competitive, that the leading instructors have built up an almost impenetrable barrier to entry by offering courses that are ridiculous in their length and scope. Every course on the entire first page of results here has over 30 hours of content.

I don't know about you, but it would take me close to a year to produce a course that large – and even then, it might not even land on the first page of search results even once the course is established.

Web development is a category I'd avoid at all costs, because the barriers to entry are just too great now. I would seek a more narrow, specific topic that might have less competition, or at least competition that can realistically be matched with a reasonable amount of effort.

It would really, really suck to spend a year creating a course only to not even make the first page of search results – and with web development, that could totally happen. Even though the topic is in very high demand, it would be a poor choice of topic for a new instructor.

It's very important to do your homework on the demand and competitive landscape for your topic before you start investing resources into it.

exercise: choose your topic

- List the topics you're qualified to teach
- Which topics have the most demand?
- Which topics have the least competition?
- What's needed to build a better course than the competition?
- Which topic presents the best opportunity?

Topic selection is perhaps the most important key to success. Take some time now to evaluate the topics you're thinking of teaching. Start by listing them out – and you might need to refer to Marketplace Insights in order to match your topics with the topics Udemy uses to categorize courses.

Research each topic with Marketplace Insights. Identify which ones have the highest demand in terms of search traffic, and how much competition you're up against in each one.

Take note of the median and maximum revenue being achieved in each topic, so you have some concrete numbers to wrap your head around.

Study the competition in the topics that seem the most promising. What's really needed to produce a course that's substantially better than what currently exists on the market? You will need to figure this out.

Should it be a longer, more comprehensive course? A course with better production values? Take note of what you need to do in order to take the top spot in that category.

After weighing the demand and competition for each topic you're considering, which one do you think presents the best opportunity? That should be the topic you produce a course on next.

CHAPTER 4 – Getting to Work

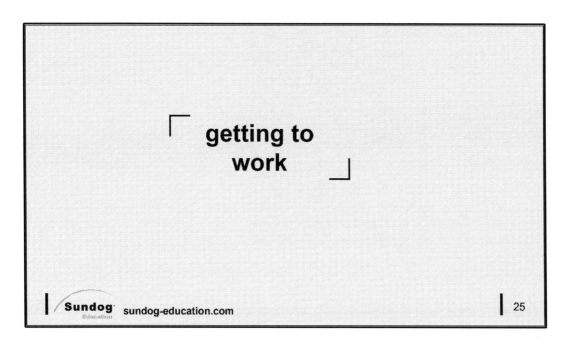

In this next section, we're going to talk about the pre-production of your course. Researching your topic, developing your course outline, materials and slides, and where to find images for your course that won't get you sued. Often, this work that happens ahead of recording is what takes the most time, and it's what makes the difference between a good course and an exceptional one. Let's get to it!

See that pile of books? Before I even wrote my outline for my best-selling course on "big data," I spent a full month reading up on all the latest developments and technologies in the field. I actually read every one of these from cover to cover, and practiced using these technologies on my own to make sure I was comfortable using them in their latest forms.

For technical topics in particular, things change very quickly. Even if you were an expert in the topic a year ago, things have probably changed so much in the past year that you have a lot of catching up to do.

It's bad enough that you're going to have to keep updating your course as the world continues to change, so don't make life more difficult than it has to be by starting off with outdated information. Some students will know if what you're presenting is obsolete information, and you'll get dinged in your reviews for it. Save everyone some trouble, and make sure you're not only an expert in the topic you're teaching – make sure you're an expert in the latest developments and emerging trends in what you're teaching as well.

One of my newer courses even has little segments called "bleeding edge alerts" where I present new technologies that haven't quite made it to the mainstream yet, but look like they have a lot of potential. This will keep that course fresh and up to date for some time to come.

By doing this research, you'll also feel more confident in the topic yourself, and that confidence will show through in your presentation of the material. Students like confident teachers who know what they're talking about!

Now that you're personally up to speed on the topic you want to teach, it's time to start applying what you yourself have learned by creating any practice materials or exercises associated with your course. I like doing this before I write the course itself, because if you can build your course around a large, single project, the process of building out that project yourself will often inform many of the little things your course needs to teach along the way.

Students do seem to like project-based courses too. If you can structure your course such that students incrementally build something substantial as they progress through it, it motivates them to complete the course. It also gives them a strong sense of accomplishment once they've finished and have something they made themselves in hand. Don't forget, happy students mean good reviews.

Don't skimp on developing hands-on activities and exercises for your course. Students, especially in technical topics, have an insatiable appetite for hands-on practice. Courses that are all theory and no practice will not fare well on Udemy. You really can't provide too much in this area; no matter how much hands-on material you provide, students will still say they want more.

For a large technical course, I might spend close to a month just developing the coding exercises for it. You also need to think about how to split up the project in a project-based course into tasks that build upon each other.

So, now we're up to two months in developing a course – one doing research, and one developing activities for it – and we have yet to even prepare a single slide yet! Putting together a comprehensive course of high enough quality to be a best-seller is a lot of hard work, and you just can't rush it.

Next, we can finally start to create an outline for your course.

> **My Ultimate, _Unofficial_ Course Creation Guide Outline**
>
> **Why should you listen to me?**
>   Financial
>   Reach
>   No prior following
> **How Udemy Works**
>   Eternal discounts
>   Volume
>   Affiliates - opting into marketing
>   Growth is slow & steady if your effort is steady
>   The element of luck
> **Topic Selection**
>   What do you know / love?
>   What are you an authority on?
>   Competitive intelligence, do they suck?
>   Has someone cornered the market with a 100-hour course?
> **Research phase**
> **Preparing course materials**
> **Course outline**

It doesn't have to be anything fancy, because you will probably end up refining it while you're recording and find issues with how different concepts flow together, or you may have second thoughts about whether some topics should be covered at all. Here's the start of the outline I wrote for this guide. I just threw it together in Google Docs.

The headers correspond to the sections in my course, and underneath each section is the list of topics I want to cover – sometimes with a few notes to myself on the specifics I have in mind for presenting them. If you prefer more formality, that's fine. Use whatever style works for you. The important thing is to have a concrete plan of the sections and lectures you need to create, so you can start chipping away at that plan.

Udemy recommends around 3-7 lectures per section, and having at least one hands-on activity in each section. They've done a lot of research on how to keep students engaged, and you'll find more recommendations from them in your course creation dashboard, under the "course structure" tab.

They also recommend mixing up your lecture formats within a section; I like to start a section with a "talking head" segment introducing it, followed mostly by screencasts. Remember it's best to keep individual lectures short; around 5 minutes or so is optimal, with each lecture only covering a single topic. The shorter, the better really. Students get a sense of accomplishment whenever they complete a lecture, and you'll deliver more of that good feeling when you have lots of short lectures. It also recognizes that many people tend to have short attention spans, and that's one way to work around that.

things your outline should have

- A "quick win"
- Udemy 101
- Priming for early reviews
- Activities, exercises, and/or quizzes in every section
- A final project, if possible
- More to explore
- Final call to action for a review
- Bonus lecture

In addition to the material you want to teach, it's a good idea for every course outline to have a few other things in it as well.

As we discussed in our own "quick win" for this guide, the very first thing you want to deliver in your course is a sense of accomplishment to your students. Start right off with having them build or create something they can be proud of, or lead right off with the most valuable piece of knowledge you have to offer. When your students are prompted for their initial thoughts about your course, you want the review they leave to be a positive one.

If you can deliver value within the first two minutes that makes them feel like they already got their $10 investment back many times over, then you'll be rewarded with exceptional review scores.

It's also a good idea to include a quick "Udemy 101" lecture to educate students on how to use the Udemy UI. Show them how they can speed up the videos if they think you're talking too slow, or slow down the videos if they think you're talking too fast. Show them how to enable closed captions if they have trouble understanding you. Show them how Udemy's Q&A feature works, so you don't get inundated with direct messages that belong in the Q&A section. If you attach resources to your lectures, show them how to find them. Doing this will avoid some negative reviews, and some questions from students who are new to the platform.

After you have about 10 minutes of lecture videos in your course, it's good to insert a small message at that point warning students that Udemy may prompt them for a review. Some students are a little confused at being asked to review a course that they've just started, and will just leave a middle-of-the-road 3-star review because they simply think it's too soon to render judgement on it. You want to be sure they know that they have the option to hit "ask me later" if they just aren't ready yet. Take care in how you phrase this message, as you need to stay within Udemy's policies. You're allowed to encourage people to leave a review, however you're not allowed to even hint that they should leave a positive one.

I usually say something like this: "Hey folks, Frank Kane here. At this point in the course, Udemy might ask you to provide an early review for it. I certainly hope you've liked what you've seen so far, and if you do have early thoughts about the quality of this course, I encourage you to leave an honest review when you're asked. If you think it's just too soon, there is a little option there to ask you again later. Don't be afraid to just hit that if you want more time to decide. And with that, let's get back to learning."

Don't use the phrase "five-star review" or it might land you in trouble with Udemy's Trust and Safety team. You have to be careful when talking about reviews with your students. Your objective is just to make sure that if they're not ready to review your course yet, they know they have the option to skip that prompt.

As we discussed earlier, students love hands-on activities. Make sure every section of your course has some opportunity for students to reinforce what you've taught, through hands-on activities, exercises, projects, or at least a quiz. If you can include a challenge for a final project in your course, all the better. You'll leave your students with a sense of big accomplishment once they're done.

When you're wrapping up your course, there are a few things you should mention. A good note to end on is by pointing them to resources for continuing their learning on the topic. You're not allowed to promote your own courses unless you're in the final "bonus lecture," but it's OK to show students some relevant books and websites as long as you're not earning affiliate commissions or anything from it.

You'll also want to make a final call to action for students to leave an honest review at the end of the course. Udemy weights reviews based on how much of the course the student has consumed upon writing it, so written reviews students leave at the end of the course count a lot toward your course's overall review score. If you've been sure to leave your students with a sense of accomplishment at the end, this can help out your review score a lot. Not many students actually make it all the way to the end of a course, but those that do have a large influence on your course's rating.

The very last thing in your outline should be your bonus lecture, and that's important enough to warrant its own slide.

the bonus lecture

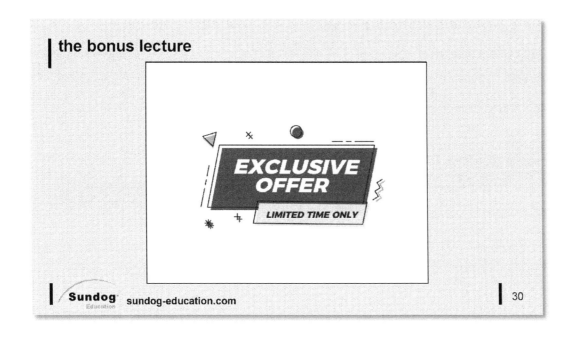

A surprisingly large number of instructors don't include a "bonus lecture" in their courses, though it's the only place in your course where Udemy allows you to present other offerings to your students. If you want to get more than $5 out of an enrollment, this is the place to do it.

A "bonus lecture" in a Udemy course must be the last lecture in the course, and must have a title that begins with "Bonus lecture." In it, you can promote any other courses you may have, or anything you want really. Maybe you want to send people to your own website, or invite them to join your mailing list. Perhaps there are consulting services you wish to tell them about, or products you sell as an affiliate. Maybe you have a companion book for the course they can buy in order to have it for future reference. Pretty much anything is fair game here.

You're not allowed to refer to your bonus lecture at any point in the course. You're also not allowed to make your bonus lecture one of your free preview lectures. Aside from that, you're allowed to break all of the self-promotion rules that apply to the rest of your course in this final lecture.

There are some best practices I can advise. Make sure whatever you are promoting is relevant to the course your bonus lecture is within, and start off promoting the thing that's most relevant.

If I have a book version of the course they just took for sale, then I'll promote that first in my bonus lecture. If I have several courses to offer, I'll try to direct them to the one that is the best follow-on to the course they just took. Don't just throw up a link to your website and make the student figure out which course or product they want; give them the most specific guidance you can on how to buy the most relevant thing from you now that they've finished your course.

Unfortunately, the vast majority of your students will not complete your course, no matter how engaging it is. So, temper your expectations of the bonus lecture's results. It will be viewed infrequently, and most students who do view it won't buy anything. But it's a way to market your other offerings automatically as students complete your course, so there's really no reason not to do it. The few minutes it takes to produce a bonus lecture will be worth it if even one student acts on it. You should also keep it short – students have low attention spans to begin with, and they'll be even lower when they know you're trying to sell them something. Stress why your offer is relevant to them and how it's the logical next step in their learning journey with you. If you need to refer students to a URL, be sure to include it in the resources for that bonus lecture.

Oh, and please respect the intelligence of your students. Don't get all high-pressure with "limited time special offers" and cheesy stuff like that. Udemy students are bombarded with stuff like that every day, and they're sick of it.

Respect your students, and maybe they'll respect you back and purchase more of your courses and other offerings in return.

This would be a good time to write, or refine, the outline for the course you plan to produce next. Start with the curriculum of the course itself, starting with the main sections you wish to cover. Under each section, list the series of short video topics you'll need to cover in order to teach the objective of that section.

If you can, try to tell a story as your course progresses – have the student build something concrete, one step at a time, as they work their way through it. At least ensure that your outline makes sense, and every video builds upon the skills learned in previous videos. Look at the curriculum from the standpoint of a new students, and make sure you're not assuming they know everything you know. Some fundamental skills may need to be covered early in your course, before you get to the stuff that you find personally interesting.

Then, go back and add the extra things we talked about: a quick win, a bonus lecture, Udemy 101, calls to action for reviews, and lots and lots of hands-on practice activities.

When you're done, sleep on it, and look at it again with fresh eyes the next morning, again from the standpoint of a new students.

Your outline is the skeleton of your new course, and getting it right is essential.

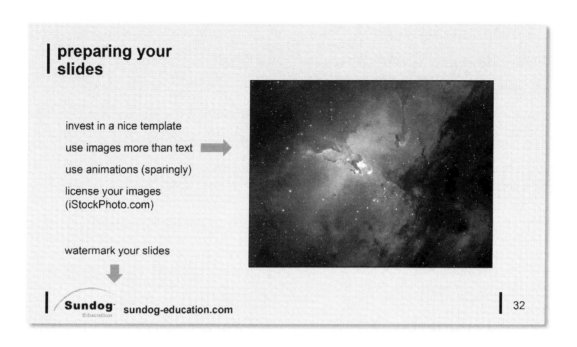

Although a lot of people bemoan the existence of PowerPoint, slide-based presentations are still the norm for presenting information in a concise way to your students. There are some general tips you can follow to make sure your students don't suffer "death by PowerPoint," and to make sure your slides are visually engaging.

First of all, it's worth investing in a professionally designed slide template. The standard ones that come with PowerPoint in particular are pretty dull. There are marketplaces such as Envato where you can license templates for your presentation software that are designed by real graphic designers with a modern look and feel. That's where I got the template for this book and my other more recent courses. It really makes a ton of difference in how professional everything looks, and it's an investment that will pay for itself quickly.

There's nothing worse than a course where the instructor is just reading each slide, word for word. To prevent yourself from doing that, make heavy use of images in your slides, and use text very sparingly. If there are some key points that would benefit from being reinforced with a minimal amount of text, I'll include some, such as I'm doing in this slide. Usually, you're better off giving students a compelling picture to look at while they listen to you explain the concept behind it. You can have the occasional list of bullet points, but slides like that should be the exception, not the norm.

Learn how to use animations in your slides, as they can help to grab the students' attention. Don't overdo it however, that just comes across as amateurish.

Perhaps the most important thing is to make sure that the images you are using are either properly licensed, or images you created yourself. You can't just copy images off of the Internet and use them because you credit their source. You are making money from your course, and if the people who created the images you stole find out about it, they will have a legitimate claim to sue you and take all of that money from you – and perhaps even more than that.

In the United States, unauthorized use of copyrighted material can result in statutory damages up to $150,000 per infringement. For every image you include in your course that you don't own, you are risking $150,000 of your money. I'm going to pause for a moment to let that sink in. Got it? Using images in your course that aren't yours is taking a huge and foolish risk that can literally ruin your life.

Also, don't think you're safe using those "free image" sites like PixaBay or searching Google Images for images that are tagged as OK for re-use. Sometimes people upload copyrighted photos to these sites even if they don't own them, so there's no guarantee that the images you're getting really are legal to use. I was once sued for using an image from a free image site on my website, because I didn't read the fine print about how exactly I was supposed to credit the photographer – and it cost me thousands of dollars to settle the case, in addition to the legal fees I incurred. There are people who set up traps like this on the Internet to fool people into using images thinking they are free, and then they go and sue them. Really, don't mess around with this.

So where do you get images from that won't get you sued? I subscribe to a website called iStockPhoto.com. They offer subscription plans that allow you to use a certain number of images every month in your courses, and since you're paying for it, you can prove that you purchased a license for these images if anyone tries to sue you for them. iStockPhoto.com also offers some legal indemnity to provide even more protection for you. Licensing images can seem like a large expense when you're creating a large course, but this is really a case where you have to spend some money to make some money. The only other alternative is to use photos and illustrations you created yourself, and in fact that's what this image is – a picture of the Eagle nebula I took using my own telescope once. I made it, so I own the rights to it.

Finally, Udemy allows you to include a small "watermark" on your slides that indicate your ownership of them, and even a link to your website, as long as it isn't too intrusive. This is a way to let students know about your website outside of the bonus lecture, and it also makes it that much more difficult for an unethical student to steal your slides and sell them as his or her own work.

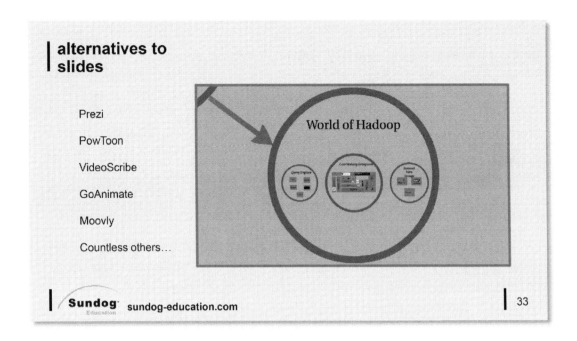

There are alternatives to slides you can use as well. I use a tool called Prezi sometimes in my courses, which lets you create animations like this one where you zoom into information that has a nested, hierarchical arrangement. It's a non-linear way of presenting information, and more engaging. I use it sparingly, however, because it can be fatiguing to watch for long periods of time.

There are also a ton of animation tools out there, such as PowToon, VideoScribe, GoAnimate, and others. This lets you create cute little animations of people doing and saying things.

You need to think about whether that sort of style is consistent with the topics you're teaching, however. While character animations might be engaging for a short promo video, it's hard to imagine how they can be used to effectively convey highly technical topics.

These tools have a fairly steep learning curve, as well. Used sparingly however, they may be a way to add a little spark of visual interest to an otherwise mundane course.

If your goal is to create more student engagement however, adding more hands-on activities to your course is probably a better bet than adding fancy animations to it.

If you do use one of these tools in your course, make sure you check the licensing terms to ensure you're allowed to use them to create content you're profiting from. At a minimum, you will probably need a paid account to use them in this manner.

> ## to script or not to script?
>
> Something to consider is fully scripting out every word you'll say in your course, while you're putting together the slides. For shorter courses such as this one, I tend to write everything out in the notes section of PowerPoint. It does increase the amount of time it takes to prepare a course substantially, but this approach comes with several benefits.
>
> First, it makes the actual recording of the course really easy. Once it comes time to record this slide, all I have to do is read the notes attached to it in PowerPoint.
>
> It also vastly reduces all the filler words like "um" and "ah," and prevents you from repeating yourself unnecessarily. It makes sure you use grammar that makes sense. And it makes sure you convey exactly the information you want to convey, while it's all still fresh in your mind while you're creating the slides.
>
> Sundog sundog-education.com | 34

Something to consider is fully scripting out every word you'll say in your course, while you're putting together the slides. For shorter courses such as this one, I do tend to write everything out in the notes section of PowerPoint. It does increase the amount of time it takes to prepare a course substantially, however this approach comes with several benefits.

First, it makes the actual recording of the course really easy. Once it comes time to record this slide, all I have to do is read the notes attached to it in PowerPoint. I have a dual-monitor setup which allows this to work well. If you don't have dual monitors, you can also just print out the notes and refer to them on paper while recording.

It's just a relief to not have to think during the recording phase of the course, since you have enough to think about making sure the recording goes smoothly from a technical standpoint.

It also vastly reduces all the filler words like "um" and "ah," and prevents you from repeating yourself unnecessarily. It makes sure you use grammar that makes sense. And it makes sure you convey exactly the information you want to convey, while it's all still fresh in your mind while you're creating the slides. Basically, it ensures that your students are getting exactly the right information in as concise a manner as possible.

It also makes it easier to produce quality captions or transcripts of your course. If you use a service such as rev.com to produce captions, you can provide them with a script to make sure they get those captions 100% correct. The jury's out on how much of an impact quality captions have on a course's sales or reviews, but certainly some students value them.

And finally, it makes it relatively easy to convert your online course into a physical book. That's something you can upsell your students on later on, or maybe even expose your course to a larger audience. Some people prefer to learn by reading instead of watching, and creating a book version of your course based on the script you wrote for it can expose it to those people.

Preparing the slides for your course may be the most time-consuming part of creating a course. I don't really expect you to stop reading right this moment and go complete all of your slides right now!

But at this point you *should* have an outline for your course, and turning that outline into slides will be a pretty straightforward task. What I want you to do is to at least select and purchase a good template that you will use for your slides. Modify it to include a watermark to identify each slide as your own work. At least create the first few slides, just to overcome that inertia of getting started on it.

Once you've got a slide deck that you're working with, adding more to it over time becomes a less intimidating task. Then, we can talk about how to turn those slides into videos.

CHAPTER 5 – Recording Your Course

So you're all ready to start recording. Odds are though, you're not a professional videographer. Most instructors learn what works and what doesn't through trial and error, and so did I at first. Let me show you the setup and techniques I've settled on, and the mistakes I made along the way so you can avoid them.

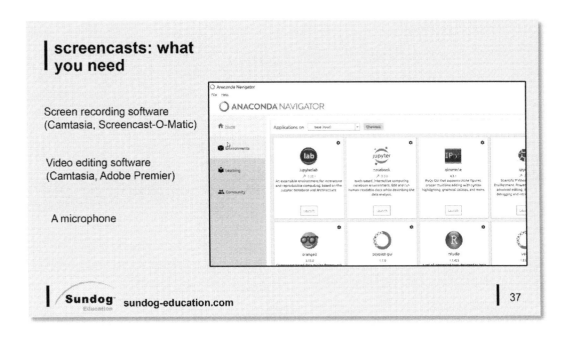

Let's start with how to record screencast lectures, as that's the easier thing to deal with. It doesn't take much to be able to record your screen while you narrate what you're doing, and for technical and perhaps other types of courses, it's possible to produce your entire course in this manner.

All you need is some software that can record your screen, video editing software so you can edit out all your mistakes, and a decent microphone.

For software, I use a product called Camtasia, and it's quite popular with online instructors. It's nice because it combines screen recording capabilities with a very capable and easy to use video editor, and also includes a plugin for PowerPoint that makes it easy to record narrations over PowerPoint slides as well. That's what I'm doing right now. Camtasia isn't too expensive, but it's not cheap either.

For a less expensive alternative, I've heard good things about a product called Screencast-O-Matic. If you're on a really tight budget, you might want to check it out. Something called OBS (Open Broadcaster Software) also gets mentioned sometimes.

Unless you're able to do an entire lecture perfectly in a single take, you're also going to need some sort of video editing software. Camtasia can also serve this role, and it has served me well throughout my entire online education career thus far.

A more professional package would be Adobe Premier, which is available as a monthly subscription – however it does have a steeper learning curve than Camtasia. Editing software is something you're probably going to have to spend some money on. I've heard some people mention DaVinci Resolve as a free alternative, but I think it comes with a lot of caveats. Sometimes you have to spend a little money in order to make money, and I consider purchasing a decent video editing package to be one of those times.

Perhaps the hardest decision new instructors seem to face is which microphone to buy, so let's spend a little more time on that.

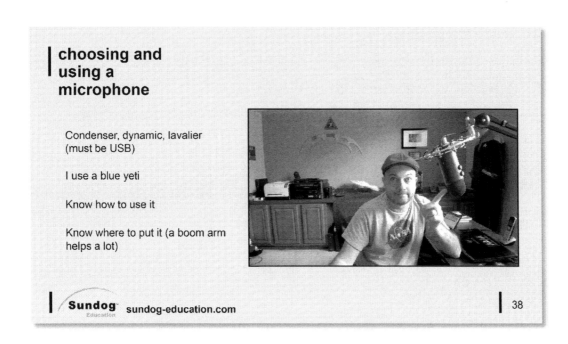

There are a LOT of microphones on the market with a huge range of prices and technical specifications. How do you know which one is right for you?

If you're going to be using a microphone to record screencasts, it will save you a lot of trouble if it is a USB microphone. That means a microphone that plugs directly into the USB port of your computer, which will allow you to record your audio and the video from your screen together at the same time, into a single video file. It is possible to buy interfaces to connect other microphones to a USB port, but it's really an unnecessary amount of expense and complexity for what you're doing. It's a lot simpler to just get a microphone made to plug right into your computer's USB port, and that narrows down the choices quite a bit right away.

Beyond that, there are fundamentally two different kinds of microphones: condenser, and dynamic. Condenser microphones are generally what are used in real recording studios. They are very sensitive and can provide professional-sounding results when used correctly. They can also be relatively fragile; you wouldn't want to be throwing around a condenser mic as part of a stage show for example. For live performances, dynamic microphones are generally used instead. Not only are they more rugged, they're not as sensitive as condenser mics – so they won't pick up as much of the background noise that's present in a live setting.

Generally speaking, a condenser microphone is the right choice for recording online courses in my opinion. You'll find a lot of advocates for dynamic microphones as well, especially if you are in a very noisy environment. We'll talk about dealing with noise more shortly.

Another choice is whether to get a large microphone on a stand, or a tiny lavalier microphone that clips to your shirt. An advantage of a "lav mic" is that it's very close to your mouth, and so it picks up more of what you're saying, and less of the noise in your environment. They also tend to be inexpensive. You have to be careful not to pick up rustling as your shirt moves, which can be a little annoying since you generally don't know if that happened until you're editing your video later on.

Personally, I use a microphone called a Blue Yeti, and it's a popular choice with online instructors. You can judge the audio quality for yourself when you listen to my videos. I've seen a lot of people criticize this microphone, but if you use it properly, it can deliver great results. Using it properly is the key.

First of all, notice in the picture that I don't have the microphone pointing at me? I'm talking into the side of the microphone, on the same side that the Blue logo is on. A Blue Yeti is meant to be mounted vertically, and you talk into the side of it. Many people get this wrong, and end up just recording the echo of their voice off of their desk as a result. Whatever mic you're using, make sure you know what part of it you're supposed to be talking into. It's not always obvious.

This mic also has a couple of knobs on the back. One sets the pattern of the mic. You want to set your mic to be directional, which on the Blue Yeti is indicated by a heart-shaped, "cardioid" pattern. Omnidirectional or stereo mics will pick up too much of the noise and echo in your room; you want to make sure it's only picking up what's in front of it, which is you. So be sure your mic has a directional or cardioid pattern to choose from.

The other knob is the gain, and it's very important to set this carefully. This will involve some trial and error as you record yourself. You want your gain high enough such that your voice, when you're speaking loudly, fills up the range of the waveform in your video editor –but not so high that the waveform tops out and "clips" when you speak loudly. Setting the gain a little too low is something you can fix while editing, though you can't fix a gain that's set too high. So, take the time to dial this in properly. For me I've got the gain on my Blue Yeti set to about ¼ of the way up, however every microphone will be different.

The other thing that's hugely important is the placement of the mic. People who complain about the Blue Yeti being "too sensitive" probably just have it positioned too far away from their mouth – so it's picking up more of the room noise and echoes, and less of your voice.

There's a rule of thumb for positioning a microphone that literally involves your thumb. If you extend your thumb and pinky finger away from each other, that's the distance your mouth should be from the microphone. You can see me illustrating that in this picture.

It's also important that your microphone is at the same level as your mouth. In a desk setup, that's hard to achieve without the use of a boom arm. I use a desk boom arm from Rode attached to a shock mount from Blue, which in turn is connected to the Blue Yeti microphone itself. Without that boom arm, there would be no way to position that microphone properly. There's a reason radio stations and professional podcasters use them. Really, it's the best investment you'll make.

One other thing to notice is that I have the microphone positioned a little bit to the side of me, pointing toward me. This is so I don't end up breathing directly into the microphone. If you speak directly into the mic, you'll pick up a lot of breath noises, popping, and clicking. Just moving the microphone out of the "line of fire" from your breath is a much more effective solution than buying a "pop filter" accessory.

So, let me recap those mic placement tips, as they are really important. Get a boom arm so you can get the mic at mouth level. Position it one thumb-and-pinky distance away. Don't talk directly into the mic; position it so it's pointing at you, but off to the side a little so you're not breathing directly into it. Take great care speak into the correct part of your mic, and to adjust its gain and pattern settings correctly.

A very common question from new instructors is how to record online courses in very noisy environments. I'm afraid the answer is that you just can't.

With correct microphone placement, you can maximize the signal-to-noise ratio between you and your environment. Microphones are designed to pick up sound, and if someone's blaring a horn outside of your window, there is nothing you can do to eliminate that from your recording, and no microphone that will magically make that noise disappear. No audio editing software can filter it out after the fact, either.

Some instructors choose to use a dynamic mic instead of a condenser for this reason, which may help a little. But a properly positioned and configured condenser mic will also pick up as much of your voice and as little of the surroundings as possible.

Don't try to cover your room with acoustic panels in an effort to make it sound proof. Acoustic panels are designed to reduce echoes in a room, not to make it soundproof. It is a very expensive mistake to buy a bunch of acoustic panels for a room thinking it will isolate your room from noise. It won't. It just makes your room sound "dead" by reducing echoes in it.

If it's too noisy, you just can't record at that time. If it's always noisy where you live, it's just not going to be possible to produce courses with good audio quality. You honestly should re-think whether making online courses is the best use of your time if that's really the situation you're in. Maybe it's quieter in the early morning or late night when you live, and you can arrange your schedule so you do your recording then. If some sporadic noise does happen, like a plane flying overhead, you can always pause your recording and pick back up at the point before the noise started, and edit it out later. If the street in that picture is outside your window 24/7 however, honestly there's not much you can do about that.

screencast best practices

- Scale up the text on your screen (Windows: Display Settings / Scale and Layout)
- Record at 1920 x 1080
- Go easy on mouse movements
- Have bullet points handy to guide you
- Don't hesitate to do a re-take!
- If you mess up, pause or clap, and start again
- Zoom into areas of interest while editing

Sundog Education sundog-education.com   40

Here are a few tips I've picked up on making good screencast lectures.

* First, remember that many students will be viewing your course on a phone or some sort of smaller screen. They won't be able to read small text on your screen. Configure your computer to make the text larger.

On Windows, you can go into your Display Settings and go into the Scale and Layout section to increase the zoom level of the text on your system. Not all applications honor this setting, so you might also need to select a larger font size in whatever applications your using while recording your screen.

Generally, you want at least 14, maybe even 16-point fonts.

* Be sure to record your screen at full resolution. Udemy can display videos up to 1080p in resolution, so if your monitor is capable of 1920x1080 resolution, you should select that resolution and record in it. You can always display or convert a video at a lower resolution than what it was recorded in, but you can never make it higher resolution. So, future-proof your course and record at the highest resolution you can.

*Go easy on your mouse movements while recording. It's OK to use the mouse as a pointer, just don't flail it all over the place just for emphasis. That's just distracting.

*It's tough to script a screencast lecture if you're illustrating some sort of complex activity, but at least have some bullet points printed out in front of you to remind you of the steps you intend to follow while recording it. If you still mess up, don't hesitate to just stop the recording and start over.

Often, your first take of a screencast lecture contains lots of little mistakes, and you don't want to look like you don't know what you're doing in front of students. At least do a dry run of what you're going to show before trying to record it.

*If you make a minor mistake while recording, have a system in place to let you easily identify that mistake while editing. I just pause for a few seconds, then start over from the point before I messed up or said the wrong thing. While editing, I look for gaps in the audio waveform that alert me to a point where I need to edit something out.

Some instructors clap or make some loud noise into the microphone so they see a sharp spike in their video editor to alert them to that point that follows a mistake.

*It's also a good idea to zoom into areas of interest while you're editing the screencast video in Camtasia or whatever video editor you're using. It further helps students to see what's going on when they're using small screens, and maintains some level of visual interest as well.

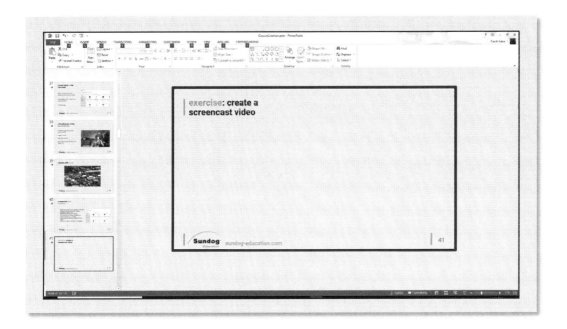

If your course outline includes screencast lectures, take the time now to try and produce one applying what you have learned.

Get the right equipment in place, and set up properly. Just practice doing it, and listen critically to your audio quality using headphones. Do you need to adjust your levels or mic placement to get the right level, and minimize noise and echoes? Take the time to get it right, and then write down exactly how you set things up so you can replicate that setup the next time.

Practice editing your screencast video to eliminate any mistakes, unexpected noises, and to zoom and pan on areas of interest as you go. Export the result, and make sure it looks good at HD resolution.

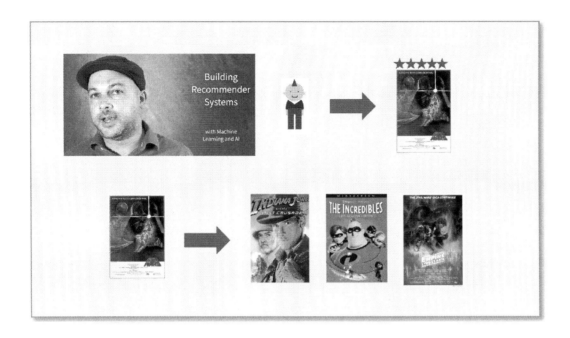

Next let's go over the technical aspects of recording "talking head" segments, such as this one.

Producing a live-action video of yourself that doesn't look amateurish is a lot more difficult than you might imagine. You don't necessarily need to have live-action segments in your courses; it's possible to create a course that's entirely slides and screencasts where you never appear in person. Well-produced "talking head" segments can help your students to see you as a relatable human being, which in theory can help your reviews and loyalty from your students when you offer new courses to them. It can set your course apart as one that has higher standards. Those higher standards also make it easier to license your course to platforms other than Udemy that are curated and are picky about what they will publish.

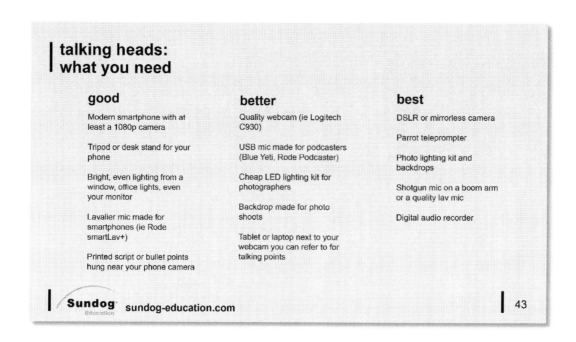

Although producing good talking head segments can be tricky, it doesn't necessarily require fancy, expensive equipment. You can get started using stuff you mostly have lying around already.

The "good" column here represents a budget-conscious start to producing good videos. If you have a somewhat modern smartphone, it probably has a surprisingly good camera built into it that's capable of 1080p or better video resolution. Why not use it to capture your video? You can buy a little desk tripod for your phone with a clip to secure your phone to it for around $10-$20.

Here's a secret: the quality of your video depends on the lighting where you are recording more so than the quality of the camera.

A well-lit scene recorded with a cell phone camera can look indistinguishable from a scene recorded with professional gear. I've even seen entire short films recorded on an iPhone, from real film-makers.

Spend some time to figure out how to light yourself evenly, and brightly enough so that your camera doesn't pick up a grainy image. If there's a window in your office, can you arrange your office so that it's in front of you while recording? Are there desk or floor lights you can move around to fill in directions of your office that are dark?

In a pinch, I've even used my computer monitor as a light source, by turning up the brightness and displaying a blank, white document on the screen. If it's close enough to your face, it can provide nice, even illumination at zero cost.

Although your phone has an adequate camera, its microphone probably isn't really up to the task of producing good results for an online course. An inexpensive option is to purchase a lavalier mic that can plug into your phone while you're recording, to take the place of your phone's built-in mic. The Rode smartLav+ is one such product, but cheaper options exist if you're conserving money. It's kind of hard to go wrong with a "lav mic".

You don't need fancy backdrops or green screens, either. Just clear out all of the junk behind you so things don't look cluttered. Ideally, you'll just have a flat-colored wall behind you, and that's just fine.

You also don't necessarily need a teleprompter. For shorter segments, maybe you can just memorize what you want to say.

You can always just print out bullet points of what you want to talk about as well, and then tape it next to your phone so you can refer to it while recording while minimizing eye movements. It's possible to keep things very low-tech and inexpensive, and still get great results.

If you have a few hundred dollars you're willing to invest, you can look at the "better" column for some ideas. Using a quality webcam such as the Logitech C930 will save you the trouble of transferring videos from your phone to your computer so you can edit and upload them. And you'll want to pair that with a USB microphone, like the ones we talked about for recording screencasts. Since lighting is so important, a battery-powered LED lighting kit can be had for surprisingly little money, and it can really improve the quality of your videos. And if a blank wall is hard to come by, a pop-up photo backdrop can be placed behind you so nobody has to see your cluttered office.

Once you've made some money from your courses, you might want to re-invest some of that into even better equipment, so your courses can be better too. This is the setup I'm using these days, and I'll go over that in more detail shortly. In brief, my setup consists of a teleprompter device attached to a DSLR camera, a shotgun mic attached to a digital audio recorder, and even more lights to play with.

Some instructors even go beyond that point, and create dedicated studios within their homes with walls painted for green-screen, acoustic paneling, fancy mixing consoles, and the whole works. That's a little too far for me, but if the technical aspect of course production is something that excites you and you have the room and budget for it – hey, I won't stop you.

As I've hinted toward a couple of times already, good lighting is really the key to good talking head segments. It doesn't matter how good your camera is – if you don't have a good lighting setup, your talking head segments are going to look amateurish.

Let's check out what some good lighting practices are.

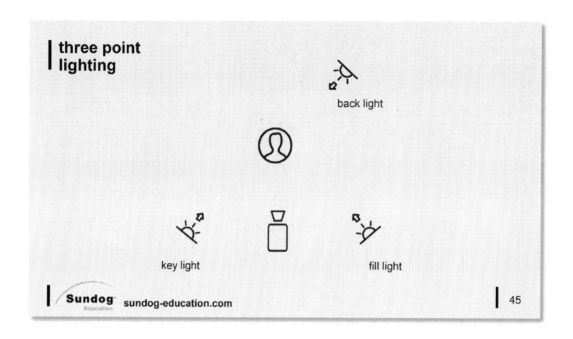

The standard setup is called "three-point lighting." The camera, of course, is in front of you, positioned straight ahead at eye level. Off to one side of the camera is your "key light," which is your primary light source. If you purchase an LED lighting kit for photographers, those lights usually allow you to adjust their intensity. The key light will probably be adjusted to light your subject brightly from one side, just not so brightly that it starts to wash out in your video. Some trial and error is needed to figure out how to adjust this properly. You also want to avoid making your key light so bright that it casts distracting shadows behind you.

The second light is the "fill light," which fills in light from the side your key light doesn't hit. A dark fill light will create deeper shadows on your subject, in sort of a "film noir" style, while brighter fill lights will provide more uniform, bright lighting.

You usually want something in the middle, in order to keep you looking bright, but still with some depth. Your fill light might just be a window on a sunny day, and that's OK.

Finally, we have the "back light." In a pinch, you could get away with not having a back light. Its purpose is to create a bit of a "halo" around you, which helps to make you pop from the background more. Keeping the back light itself out of the frame can be a little tricky; normally you'd want it above you, just outside of the frame, pointing down at the back of your neck.

The key and fill lights should be positioned at the level of your head, pointing toward you. Again, you'll have to experiment with different intensities to find the look you want, while avoiding saturation and shadows at the same time. It can be time consuming to figure out at first, but it's better to spend that time up front than to record all of your talking head segments only to find that you don't like how they look after you're done editing them all.

> ## lighting hacks
>
> - A window can serve as your fill light
> - A monitor with an empty white document can serve as your key light
> - A back light can serve double duty illuminating your background
> - To avoid shadows, stand well in front of your background
> - Experiment with different light intensities
> - Use equipment that's easy to set up and tear down
>   Such as battery-powered LED lights and pop-out backgrounds

In a cramped office, finding room for all these lights and getting them just where they need to be can be difficult or even impossible. Here are a few "hacks" you may find useful.

* If your office has a window, use it as one of your light sources. It probably makes a great fill light; position yourself with the window to one side, and your key light to the other. You can even adjust its intensity with your window blinds!

*As I mentioned before, in a pinch a bright computer monitor displaying a white, empty document can serve as a light source if it's close enough to you. If you're recording yourself sitting at your desk, this isn't an unreasonable thing to do at all, especially if you use it as a fill light.

*Sometimes a back-light can pull double duty by illuminating your background as well as you. I like to position my back-light behind me at waist level, pointing straight up. It creates a nice glow behind me, and also helps to wash out any shadows on the background.

*If you have a problem with yourself casting shadows on your background, a simple trick is to just stand further in front of the background. This will make your shadows appear less harsh, or ideally be cast outside of your frame.

*Again, it's important to be patient and experiment with different lighting settings, and look at the results, and keep iterating until you're happy with it. There's nothing worse than spending a day recording talking head segments, only to realize that there's a distracting shadow or you appear to be glowing in all of them.

*Use equipment that's easy to set up and tear down. I started off using compact fluorescent soft-boxes and umbrella lights used by photographers, and they were large, bulky, hard to set up, and required me to find an outlet to plug them into. I've since replaced them with a much simpler, cheaper LED lighting kit that's powered from batteries, and now I no longer dread setting up for talking head shoots.

Pop-up backdrops that have a built-in metal frame that pops open and provides tension for the backdrop can also save you a lot of trouble. Larger systems include two stands with a bar that you drape a sheet over, however this too is cumbersome to set up – and that sheet often has wrinkles that you can't get out. Avoid those systems for the simpler backdrops that just pop out in an instant with all the wrinkles pulled out automatically.

Getting the right framing of your shots is also really important. Generally, you want to capture yourself from the waist up. This gives you a lot of flexibility while editing, as you can fabricate "close ups" and different angles by just zooming and cropping this one camera angle in different ways.

If your camera is too close, you're only going to get a close-up of your head. If your head is filling all of the student's screen all of the time, it just comes across as creepy. That's why you want a wider angle to work with.

Make sure your camera is positioned at eye level. You want to be looking into the camera just as you'd look into the eyes of someone you're talking to. A camera above or below your eyes looking up or down just looks creepy, and you don't want creepy videos.

Also, be mindful of the extents of your backdrop. The very top of the image there is unusable because the edges of my backdrop are visible in it. Fortunately, the top of my head doesn't extend into that area, so it's a problem I can fix in editing by cropping the video.

Ideally, I would have positioned the backdrop higher, but the physical constraints of my office made that impossible.

A lot of instructors are enamored with the idea of playing with green screen. The idea is to record yourself in front of a green background. Then, while editing, you can remove that green background and replace it with whatever images you want, making you appear as though you're someplace else. It's a cool trick, but it's usually not done well. And when it's not done well, it just screams out "amateur." That's not the word you want associated with your course.

Every professional videographer and editor I've talked to has said the same thing – don't use green screen unless you have a really good reason to. If you don't have a need to make yourself look like you are someplace that you are not actually in, don't do it. Just use a neutral background of some sort. The result will be much more professional looking than if you just use green-screen for no good reason.

It's just too easy to mess up while using a green screen. First of all, the effect depends on very evenly lighting the screen behind you. Doing this often requires multiple lights and a lot of trial and error to get a uniform result. You also need to completely eliminate any shadows from you on the green screen for it to work, which can require even more lights. Wrinkles in the screen can mess you up. Standing too close to the screen will result in "color bleed" that results in a green halo around you that you just can't get rid of. Hair is tough to get right.

Fast motions of your hand against the green screen will look blurry and the green of the screen will bleed into them. If you have green eyes or any green in your clothing, that will also mess up the effect.

Even if you get all of that right, it can be tough to choose a background to replace the green screen that matches the camera angle you shot yourself from. There are just a million ways to screw it up, and it's simply not worth it. You're making an online course, not the next "Star Wars."

With a neutral background, you can still overlay graphical elements beside you in editing as needed, and keep the focus on you and those elements instead of some fancy background that doesn't really exist.

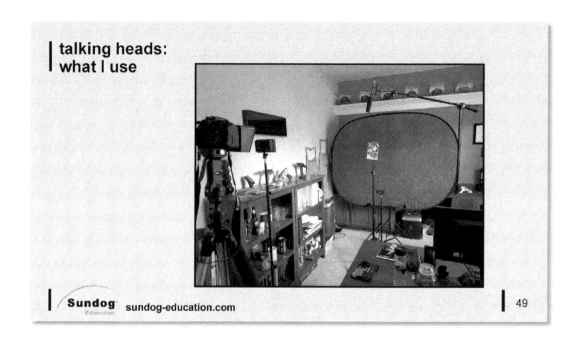

I've experimented with a lot of different setups and gear over the years, so next I'll talk about the specific setup I've settled on for talking head segments.

As we discussed, there are less expensive ways to get started, but if you have several hundred dollars that you're willing to invest and you already have a good camera for photography, this might be a setup you want to emulate.

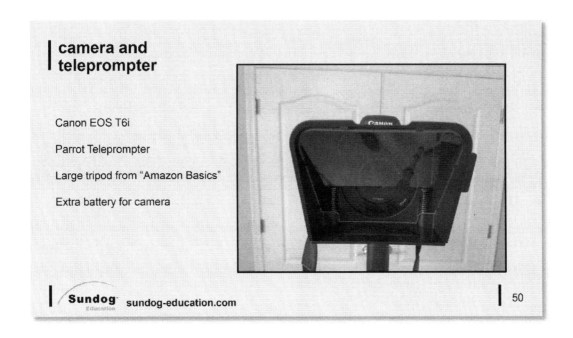

Let's start with the business end of my setup – the camera. I already owned a DSLR camera for photography, and it turns out any DSLR or mirrorless camera can also do a good job of recording short video segments as well. I have a Canon EOS T6i camera, though the specific make and model is unimportant. As long as it's a camera with removable lenses that can record 1080p movies or better, you're in business.

A spare battery for your camera is also a good investment, so you can always have one ready that's fully charged. They can chew through batteries pretty quickly when recording movies.

I chose a short 40mm lens, since it enables cool depth of field effects – but this isn't so important if you have a backdrop behind you. What's more important is to use a lens that allows you to achieve the proper framing of you from the waist up, within the space confines of where you are shooting. The camera is attached to an inexpensive tripod from "Amazon Basics." You need to be sure to get a tripod that's tall enough to reach your eye level; many of them are not, unless you're really short. So, check the height of a tripod before you buy one.

Finally, attached to the camera is a teleprompter device. It's a relatively simple and inexpensive device called a Parrot Teleprompter. It screws onto the front of the camera lens, and has a clip on the bottom that you slide your cell phone into. The idea is that you install their app on your phone, sync it to scripts that you upload into DropBox, and then you can play back those scripts in their teleprompter app.

The device itself reflects the text of that script onto the front of the teleprompter so you can read from it, while still looking directly into the camera and without moving your eyes while you read. Through some magic of physics, the camera doesn't see the text, but you do.

The Parrot Teleprompter also has an optional Bluetooth remote control you can buy, which I highly recommend. It allows you to start, stop, position, speed up, or slow down the text while you are recording. It makes it a lot easier to do re-takes without having to walk back up to the camera, and to keep up a natural pace by allowing you to adjust the speed at which your script scrolls by.

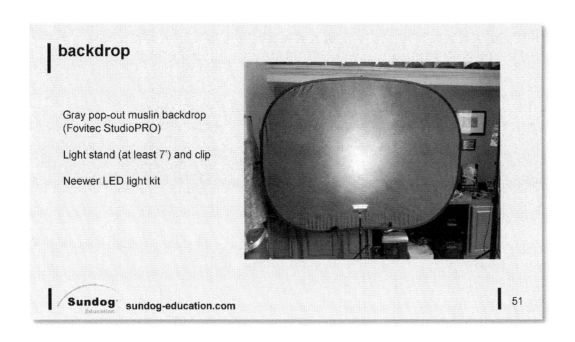

For my backdrop, I've been leaning toward this gray one lately. It's a pop-out one with a metal frame that creates tension on it, to help reduce wrinkles. To use it, it is mounted to a light stand with a special clip that's sold with the backdrop. Be sure to get a light stand at least 7 feet tall, so you can get the backdrop high enough behind you.

I have a battery-powered LED light at the bottom of the backdrop, shooting up at it. This creates a nice bright glow in the center that I stand behind, which helps to make me pop from it and to focus visual interest where I am standing. It also helps to wash out any pesky shadows on the backdrop. That light is part of a 3-light kit from Neewer that includes the lights, stands, batteries, and a charger for the batteries.

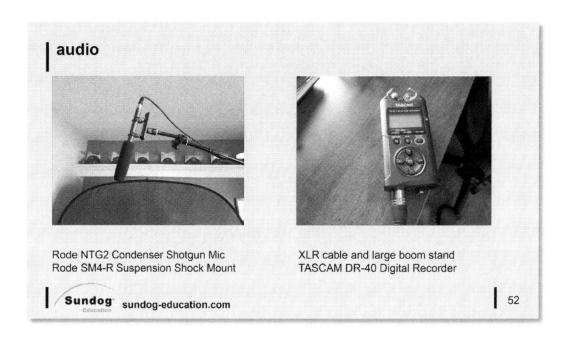

For audio, I'm using a highly directional "shotgun" mic – specifically a Rode NTG-2. The challenge, as with any mic, is getting it where it needs to be for the best audio – and for talking heads, it also needs to be positioned out of frame so you don't see it in the video.

What works best is positioning it above you, but just in front of you, pointing down toward your mouth. I've found that pointing the mic straight down so its back is facing the ceiling works best for eliminating echoes from the room. Even though it is a directional microphone, it will still pick up a lot of room noise and echo if it's not in just the right spot.

Take care not to position it directly above or behind you – it needs to be a little bit in front of you, so it can pick up the sound coming out of your mouth, and not the sound that reflected off the rest of the room and eventually above your head.

You'll need to experiment with some test video to get the mic as close as you can to your mouth, while still being out of frame.

The mic is on a large boom stand that actually cost more than the mic itself. It's a large and heavy item that's expensive to ship, so I picked up mine at a local Guitar Center store. The mic's connected to a digital audio recorder. This is a small battery-powered device that records to a little SD card, and provides power to the microphone. It's connected to the mic with an XLR audio cable.

This means that my video and audio are recorded separately. When I'm done recording my talking head segments, I have to first connect my DSLR camera to my computer to download the video. Any audio in the video from my camera has to be eliminated while editing, because I want to use the audio from my shotgun mic, not the mic in my camera.

Then I have to connect my digital audio recorder to my computer to download the audio files. After that I have to match up the audio from the shotgun mic and the video from my camera, and synchronize them in my video editing software.

Synchronizing that audio and video can be a little tricky, and that's what these clapperboards are made for! By matching up the point in the video where the clapper hits the board with the point in the audio where it makes a loud "clap", you can synchronize the audio and video in post-production more easily. If you always wanted an excuse to buy one of these, there you go.

Looking at this image, I don't look very happy, do I? The truth is that getting all this equipment set up just right all on your own can get frustrating. Once that camera starts rolling, you need to be excited, happy, and energetic.

It's a good idea to record your "talking heads" during whatever time of day you have the most energy and enthusiasm. For me, that's in the morning, just go with whatever works for you.

Notice my attire in that photo as well. I was filming a course specifically targeted at executives and business leaders, so I broke out my best sport coat and shirt for this shoot. For a more technical course, I'd wear something more informal, though still nice. Just try to look like someone your students will both relate to and respect.

I've been on a couple of real film sets, where they've even applied makeup to eliminate any shiny spots and hide the bags under my eyes that are starting to reveal my age. Some men might be a little squeamish with the idea of makeup, however it's totally normal when filming. I don't do it when filming my own courses because I don't know how to, but if someone in your household knows how to do this professionally, go for it.

A couple of more little "hacks" and tips for you…

You might wonder why I have a birthday card with Thomas the Tank Engine stuck to the top of a lighting stand here. This is a trick I use to focus my camera when I don't have anyone around to help me out. If you record with autofocus on in your camera, you'll end up with lots of distracting moments where your video becomes blurry while your camera decides to focus on some different part of you. Moving around even a little can trigger autofocus to kick in. Autofocus is your enemy. Do not use autofocus.

Instead, I use Thomas here as a stand-in for me. I'll allow the camera to focus on this card that's positioned exactly where my head will be while recording, and then turn off autofocus on my camera lens so it will not try to change the focus from that point.

I'm using a birthday card because it has lots of little text on it that makes it easy to see how well the camera is focused in its view screen when you zoom in on it.

The stand is used to position the card at the same height as my head. And the stand itself is positioned exactly where I will stand. To mark where I will stand, I have some painter's tape on the floor so I can quickly and easily stand in exactly the same position I used for focusing.

By the way, you do need to choose that position somewhat carefully. You need to stand far enough in front of your backdrop to reduce the sharpness of any shadows on it that you might cast, but close enough that your camera will still fit both you and the backdrop in the same frame nicely, from the waist up.

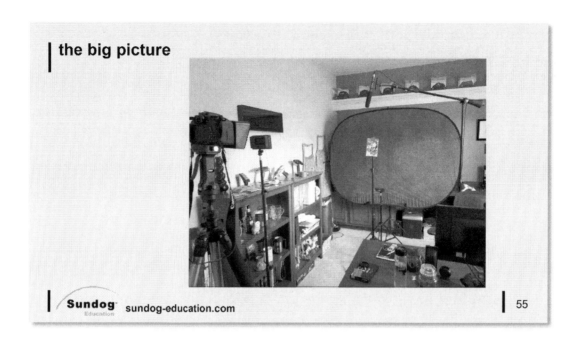

Let's step back and take a wider view of my entire setup again, and see how it all fits together.

From a lighting standpoint, you can see my key light just in front of and to the left of my camera, and the backlight that's shining up on my backdrop. I'm actually relying on my window and ceiling light, both off-camera, as my "fill light." Anything I can do to make setup easier means I'll do more recording and make more courses, which is what it's all about. The side of my teleprompter is more clearly visible there, and you can see the boom stand my shotgun mic is attached to. My stand-in for focusing is also up.

All this equipment made an office that was already pretty cluttered look even more cluttered. Students don't see any of that however – they just see a nicely lit Frank in front of a nice, clean gray background. All the chaos behind the scenes doesn't exist as far as they are concerned!

The most expensive component of this setup is the camera itself, and the nice thing about using a DSLR or mirrorless camera is that you can use it for photography when you're not using it to record talking heads, so you do get some extra value out of that investment.

The remaining equipment only totals a few hundred dollars. If you want to replicate the same setup and gear I use, it's actually not all that hard to do, go for it!

Still, as you can see producing a good talking head video requires quite a bit of work, not just while recording but also while finding all those things you need to edit. That can take some time. If your course doesn't require videos, it might be something you want to avoid at first. And that's OK. Work your way up to this when you're ready for it. You'll know when that is.

If you're new to course creation, or trying out a new setup for filming, I STRONGLY recommend using Udemy's test video service. The idea is to just send a short clip of a few minutes of you talking about anything you want to Udemy, and they will provide feedback as to the audio and video quality and things you might be able to improve. You'll find a link to submit a test video in your instructor dashboard.

It is very hard for you to objectively evaluate a video you've spent hours trying to get right. When I was starting, I uploaded some poorly produced green-screen videos that really never should have seen the light of day, and did an entire course with the audio levels way too low because I didn't know any better.

You might be a little afraid to receive criticism on your hard work, believe me though, it's better to get it from Udemy before you publish your course, than to get it from students after you've published it.

Don't produce a single lecture video until Udemy has evaluated a test video from you and given you the green light on your A/V quality. Also, make sure you can replicate the A/V setup you used for your test video in your future recordings.

Make note of your gain setting on your microphone, where exactly your microphone was, how you focused your camera, the lighting conditions, everything. Try to remember how loudly you talked and maintain as much consistency as possible with the final test video Udemy approved.

Use Udemy's test video service, and act upon their advice. Unless they say "it's perfect!" there is room for improvement. Udemy has become a highly competitive marketplace, and poor A/V quality is pretty much a guarantee of poor sales of your course.

CHAPTER 6 – Post-Production

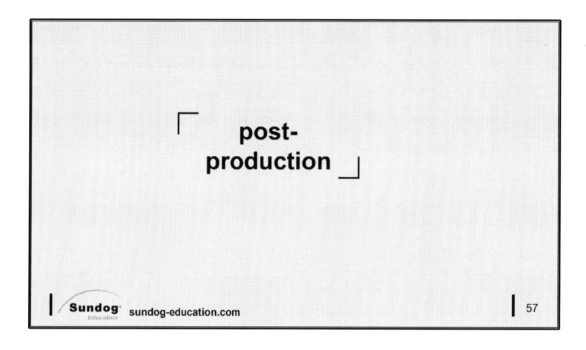

Recording your lecture videos is really less than half of the work in producing them. You need to clean up your raw recordings in the editing pass, and upload them into your course curriculum in Udemy. Let's talk about ways to make that process as efficient as possible.

The first step is to import your raw recordings into whatever video editing application you've settled on. I use Camtasia, which is shown here. You can see I've imported a screen recording from some PowerPoint slides, followed by a screen recording of me writing some code. This isn't a course on how to use Camtasia, but it's pretty intuitive for the most part.

The timeline is where you drag your media clips into what will become your final production. You can see two tracks there; the bottom one is the video and the top one is the audio. If you captured your video using Camtasia, these will be split into two different tracks, but the audio and video might be combined into a single track if you captured it via other means.

You can see the highlighted portion is a lengthy screencast session, with a short slide-based introduction in front of it. The little pointy thing above the tracks selects what point in the edited video you're looking at right now; currently it's at 0 seconds, and showing the very beginning of my slide deck. As you drag that pointy thing around, you can jump around to different parts of your video to work with.

Take a look at the audio waveform in track 2 and you'll see there's a lot of empty space that needs to be edited out. Some of that's me waiting for my computer to finish some operation, and some of it's because I messed something up, paused, and re-started a section of the lecture. It needs to be edited to produce a video that students will find engaging. Before going any further though, sit down and ask yourself if you really just need to re-record the lecture entirely. If you messed up too much, or found yourself repeating yourself and using lots of filler words like "um," "like", and "you know" – it's probably best to just record another take of it before you invest time in editing it. Editing can only fix so much.

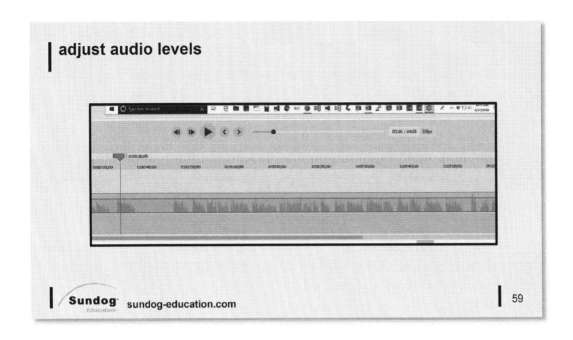

The first thing I do is adjust the audio levels. You'll have to do this for every clip you've imported into your project, and do it consistently. I just eyeball it, and grab the line in the audio track and drag it up with my mouse until the loudest parts of the waveform are almost, but not quite, hitting the top of the track. It should look something like this when you're done. Be careful; if your audio is too low, students will complain about it. If you drag it up too high, the louder parts will clip out and sound terrible.

Notice how none of my audio actually hits the top of the track where it would max out and clip. If there is more than one clip in your project, it's a good idea to listen to the transitions between each clip to make sure it sounds natural and at the same level. You don't want the audio in your final video to suddenly sound louder or quieter for no reason – that just screams "amateur."

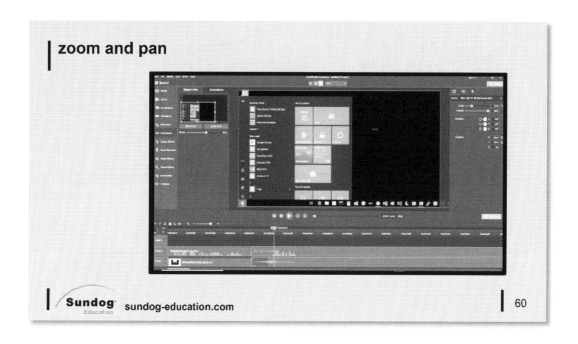

Next, I'll play through the entire video from the beginning, just cleaning everything up and polishing it as I go. As a result, you can expect to spend a lot more time editing a video than it took to actually record it. You sort of have to be in the right frame of mind to do it as it can seem tedious after a while.

Some instructors hire people to help them with editing, however it's hard for someone who isn't familiar with your topic to know which things should be emphasized and what constitutes a mistake that needs to be edited out. I still do it myself for that reason, unless it's something really complex and highly-produced like a promo video.

As I'm working my way through the video, I use Camtasia's "Zoom and Pan" feature to zoom in on screencast videos to highlight the part of the screen I'm working with.

Some very successful instructors don't do this in order to streamline their editing, but I think it's helpful especially for students viewing your device on a small screen. In Camtasia, you'll find this under the "Animation" tab on the left, and then there's a "Zoom-n-Pan" tab at the top there.

All you do is move the playback head (the "pointy thing" in the timeline) to the point where you want to zoom in on something, and drag the selection frame in the small preview window on the left – the window under "Zoom-n-Pan" – to focus in on the part of the screen you want to show.

This is a little counter-intuitive; you don't adjust the frame in the large preview window, it's the smaller one on the left where you zoom and pan.

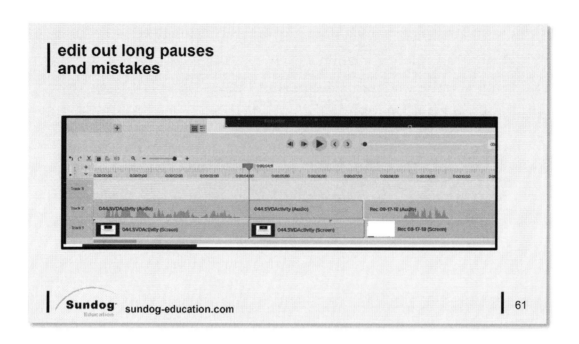

The other task is to edit out any long pauses or mistakes. In either case, you move the playback head to the beginning of the area you want to edit out, and click the "split" icon above the timeline – that's the one just to the left of the magnifying glass there that's used to zoom in or out of the timeline – to create a split point in the timeline. Then you create another split at the end of the area you want to edit out, select the section you just created in between the two splits, and delete it. You have to select everything to the right of the section you edited out, and drag it to the left so it takes the place of that section.

If you're editing out some long operation that you just don't want to force the student to have to sit there and watch, I usually use a flip transition at the point where I edited out that content in order to signal to the student that time has passed there.

If I'm editing out some sort of mistake where I just stopped and re-started a portion of the lecture, I try to make that as un-noticeable as possible. While editing things out, be careful to split things at points where the audio waveform is at zero, otherwise you'll hear a distracting cutoff. You'll also want to try and maintain a natural pacing of your speech; don't jam two words together where you would normally have stopped to take a breath.

Things I don't do are editing out breaths themselves, editing out mouth noise, or attempting to reduce noise in the audio. That's because I was careful to position my microphone in such a manner to reduce those effects as much as possible.

Editing video is very tedious work, and the more you can address issues at their source instead of at the editing stage, the faster your course production will go.

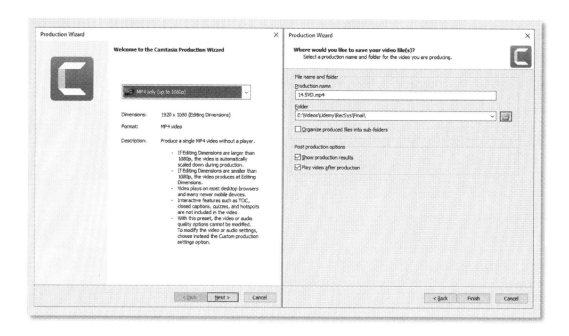

Once you've worked your way through the entire lecture, it's time to export it as an MP4 that you can upload into Udemy or any other platform.

Note that I captured and produced my video at 1920x1080 resolution. Even though Udemy doesn't always offer 1080P resolution to students, it would be foolish not to give them full HD-quality video. They can always down-sample it to lower resolutions, but you can never create higher resolution video from a lower resolution. Even 1080 might be considered low resolution in a few years, so produce your video at the highest resolution you can to make it as future-proof as possible.

In Camtasia, I just select "MP4 only (up to 1080p)" in the production wizard after hitting the "share" button to produce my final video. On the next screen, take care to un-check "organize produced files into sub-folders," since it's silly to have a sub-folder for each individual MP4 file.

It's a good idea to play the resulting video when it's done exporting and double check that it seems OK, especially when you're a beginner at video production. It's easy to miss things while editing, and one extra check can't hurt.

Do try and keep things up to date and organized; I name my video files with their lecture number first so they'll sort in the correct order when I view them all together, and put them all in a folder that's just for the final edits of my videos.

back it up!

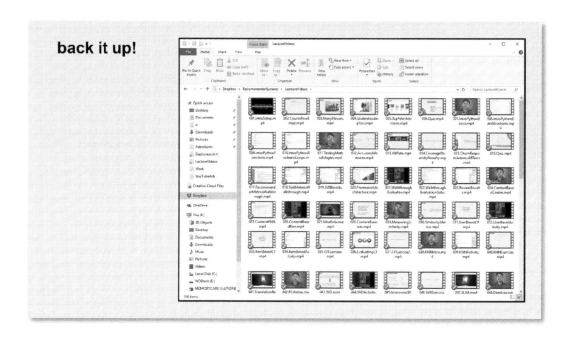

Your final videos are your most important asset, and it's a matter of time before your computer breaks. So back them up someplace safe. At a minimum, save them to an external hard drive or thumb drive that you won't lose. It's even better to copy them into some cloud-based backup service such as Dropbox or AWS Glacier or something, so your videos will be safe even if something happens to your home, and you'll have access to them while travelling too. I use Dropbox myself, though it's only because I was already using it for other stuff and I was familiar with it.

Better still, back them up in more than one place, because you never know when Dropbox will go away either for that matter. Udemy will re-process your videos and add a Udemy watermark to them once you upload them into your platform. There's no way to retrieve your original videos from Udemy, so it's up to you to keep them safe and backed up someplace.

upload it

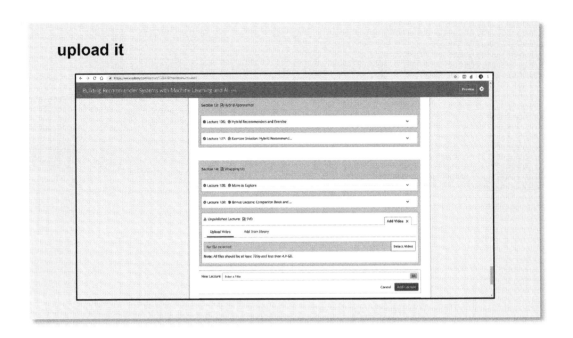

Finally, you'll upload your finished videos into Udemy's course creation UI. This is under the "Curriculum" tab in the editing screen for your course, once you've created the course itself.

I don't want to spend a lot of time on how to use Udemy's user interface because you can learn that on Udemy itself; it's the stuff they don't tell you that I'm focusing on here.

There's no need to save your work as you develop your curriculum; everything is saved automatically as you go. Nothing will be visible to students until you submit your course for review and it's published on the marketplace, so don't worry about keeping things perfect as you build up your course. Nobody can see it but you, unless you have explicitly made it visible.

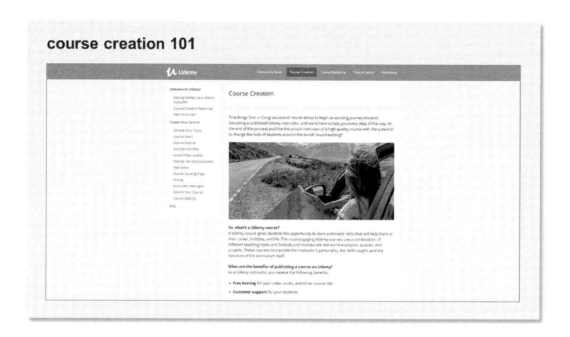

If you are brand new to Udemy, some of the basics that I'm *not* covering will be found in the "Teach Hub" section of their website. Just go to https://teach.udemy.com/ and it will direct you to Udemy's own, free resources on how to create a good course. Udemy has a lot of knowledge about instructional design and A/V production that they've shared here, and that's what they are experts at. It's the stuff I've learned through experience as an actual instructor that I'm aiming to share here.

If you have questions about the mechanics of course creation, please check Udemy's own content first. In some cases, they'll even direct you to short, free courses of their own that they have produced.

For example, they offer free courses on how to use some of their special lecture types, such as assignments and coding exercises. If you're interested in using these features, I'll just refer you to these.

Assignments, coding exercises, and quizzes are all ways to create more student interaction with your course. They require students to either submit their work for evaluation, or take an online multiple-choice quiz to reinforce what they have learned. This sort of interactivity is important from an instructional design standpoint, and by all means your course should include as many hands-on activities as possible.

However, you might want to think twice before including features such as these into your course. There are a couple of big downsides to using them – one is that it will lock you into Udemy's platform, unless you also create video-based versions of these exercises for use on other platforms.

Remember that you own your course, and you're simply licensing it to Udemy. If you want to upload your course to other platforms as well, you won't be able to do that if it depends on special lectures types that only exist within Udemy.

The other downside is that they can create more work for you as an instructor. If students submit their work through the assignments feature, they might expect you as an instructor to evaluate their work and provide feedback.

This sounds like fun, until you get to a point where you have thousands of students and can't keep up with all that work. Remember that on average, you'll be lucky to receive $5 from an individual student enrollment, and at some point, you have to ask yourself if "grading their work" as they go through your course is worth $5. Your time has value, and with enough students that time can become significant.

Instead, I keep all of my content in the form of MP4 videos and supporting materials that can be downloaded from my own website. If your entire course can be represented with a collection of MP4's and a URL to your course materials, then that course will be portable to any online learning platform.

I still have lots of activities and exercises in my courses, but they are in video form. I'll have one lecture video that describes the exercise to the student and asks them to try it on their own. Then in the next lecture video, I'll review my own solution to the exercise so they can compare it with their own.

I only use quizzes early in the course when the student hasn't learned enough to do an entire project on their own, but I even keep these video-based. I'll just show a question on each slide, give the student a moment to think up their own answer, and review the answer on the next slide. It's not as "interactive" as Udemy's quiz feature, however it's more portable, and allows more flexibility as well. Udemy's quiz feature only supports multiple-choice quizzes where there is only one correct answer per question. If you're presenting your own quiz in video form, you can do whatever you want. It's not as interactive since students aren't actually clicking on an answer, but if you intend to publish your course outside of Udemy, it's kind of the only way to go.

If you do only intend to publish your course on Udemy, then by all means experiment with assignments, coding exercises, and quizzes using their platform. It really is the right thing to do from an instructional design standpoint, though it means going all-in with Udemy.

CHAPTER 7 – Udemy SEO Tips

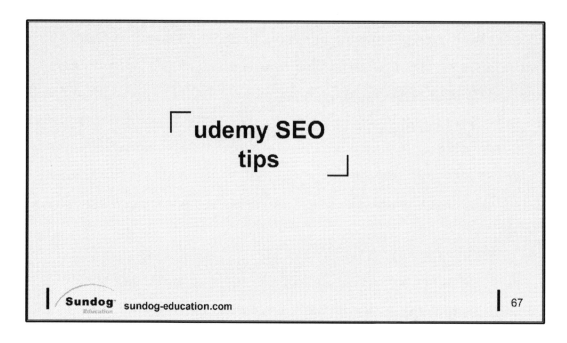

Producing a great course won't do anybody any good if they can't find it, so you need to make sure your course landing page is designed to grab the attention of Udemy's search engine, and the attention of potential students once they find it. Let's talk about the world of SEO, or search engine optimization, on the Udemy platform. A little extra effort on your landing page can go a very long way.

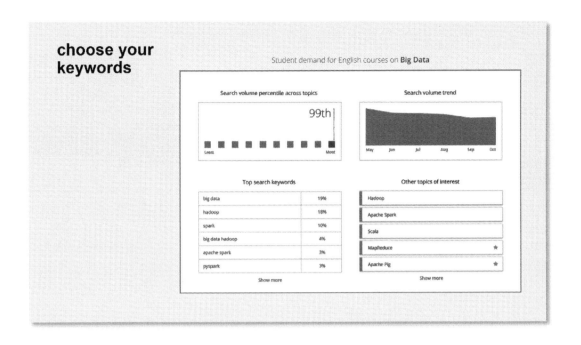

The first step in any search engine optimization effort is to figure out which keywords you are trying to optimize for. A rookie mistake is to search Udemy for your course's title, and figure out which "page" you're on of search results based on that. Students aren't going to be searching for your course title; they're going to be searching for specific skills that they want to learn.

You need to think about the students most likely to buy your course, and what words they are likely to be searching for, assuming they've never heard of you or your course before. The words your potential students are searching for are your keywords, and you'll want to make heavy use of them on your course landing page.

Most courses can be described by many different keywords, and you have to figure out which ones are the most important to focus on.

Fortunately, the same Marketplace Insights tool in Udemy's instructor dashboard that we used for selecting your topic can also be used for keyword research. I have a course about "big data", but people refer to that by many different names. For example - Spark, Hadoop, and MapReduce. I can select each of those topics in Marketplace Insights and compare their search volume against each other. That lets me figure out how valuable each potential topic is.

Even more valuable is the "top search keywords" below that. This is telling you in no uncertain terms which terms students searched for who bought a course in this given topic. So, the top search keywords in the top topic that applies to your course are the keywords you should be focusing on.

The "other topics of interest" can also give you ideas of other topics you might not have even considered. For example, I forgot that people might be searching for "Scala," and that's worth exploring as well to see if it also has a high search volume. If so, I'd consider its top search keywords as well.

This little exercise shows that a course in the Big Data topic should of course have "big data" as a keyword, as well as "Hadoop" and "Spark." Your goal is to capture as many of the top keywords relevant to your course in your course landing page as possible.

Your course title is hugely important from both an SEO and a conversion perspective. You want to capture as many of the top keywords as you can in your title, but the title still needs to be compelling and capture the attention of students. You can't just stuff all of the keywords into it and expect students to be drawn to it once they actually read it.

There are three components to a good course title that I've identified. The first component is the keywords. Remember that the top two search terms for the "big data" topic were "Big Data" and "Hadoop," and I've made sure that both of those terms are part of my title. You have to work them in somehow. It's not just Udemy's search algorithms that you're making happy, students are going to be more likely to click on your course if it contains the *terms* they were searching for in the first place.

Next, we need to somehow differentiate your course from all of the others in your category. At the time this book was created, most technical courses were very heavy on theory and light on practice, so the phrase "Hands-On" conveyed that this one would be very much focused on *doing* and not just learning. The word "ultimate" conveys its comprehensive nature.

Remember all courses generally cost the same amount on Udemy given their frequent fixed-price promotions, and given the choice between a comprehensive course and a narrowly-focused one, they'll generally choose the comprehensive course. If you can use words like "Ultimate," "Complete," "A-Z", or "Zero to Hero" in your course title, that tends to go over very well with Udemy students.

If you look at the top-selling courses on Udemy, many of them use these phrases in their titles, and that's not a coincidence. You need to earn the use of words like that; a course that's under 10 hours in length will have a hard time calling itself "Ultimate" compared to competing courses.

Finally, we want our title to tell a story about what the student will be able to achieve after taking your course. Convey the results your course will deliver and the problem it will solve for your students. That's what students really care about. "Tame your Big Data" is how I tried to capture that in the few remaining characters I had left in the title.

Remember Udemy policies, though – you're not allowed to make any monetary or financial promises in your course title. I couldn't use the phrase "Make a Million Dollars" in the description of a course like this on Udemy for example. Nor would I want to, because that would be deceiving.

So again – your title needs to contain at least the top two keywords for your topic, it needs to convey some sort of differentiation from your competition, and it needs to tell a story about the results your students will achieve from your class. That's a lot to pack into a short title, but it's an effort worth making.

Udemy allows you more room for your course's subtitle. Repeating a keyword you really want to rank highly on is a good idea here; in my case, I've repeated "Hadoop" as it's an important keyword for my course, even though it's already in the title. There is a bit of keyword stuffing going on here, as I've listed the most popular technologies that my course covers, and I want to be sure that people who search for those technologies at least see my course. I've still made sure to make it somewhat compelling to a human reader as well; it's phrased in such a way as to convey the comprehensiveness of the course.

Look at all the topics we cover! The list goes on!

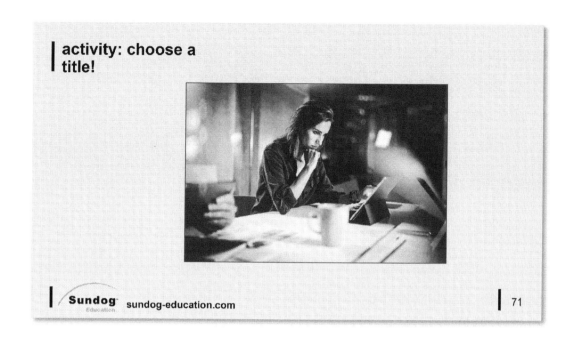

Choosing the right title and subtitle for your course is really important for its success. While these ideas are still fresh in your head, take a moment to write down some ideas for the perfect title and subtitle for your next course. If you have existing courses on Udemy, re-evaluate their titles and see if they can be better.

Give that a shot before moving on with the book.

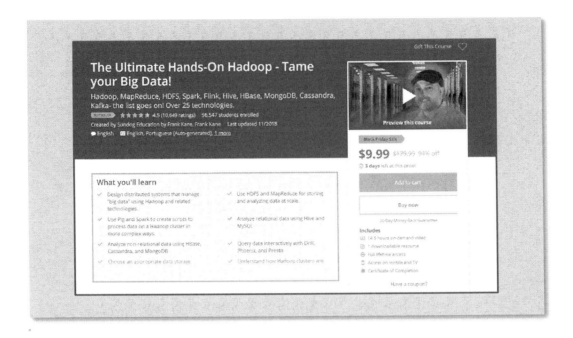

Take a look at a course landing page from a student's perspective, and it'll help you understand what you need to focus on to optimize the conversion of your course. It's not just Udemy's search algorithms you're trying to make happy, it's also Google – and they tend to prioritize content that's "above the fold" of your course landing page. That's also what students focus on when they are evaluating your course, so making all of the stuff that's visible on your course landing page as compelling as possible is good for SEO, and good for conversion rates too. We talked about the title and subtitle already, which are two of the first things a student sees.

But look at what's just below that: "What you'll learn." This content is buried in Udemy's landing page creation UI, and it's more important than anything else other than the title! You need to expend a good amount of effort to ensure that the skills students see under "what you'll learn" match up with the skills they are trying to gain. And the order you present them in matters, too.

These items exist in your course editing screen under the "Target Student" tab, and then you have to scroll down to the section labeled "What will students achieve or be able to do after taking your course?"

As with the title, you want to write these from the angle of skills your students will gain, and problems they will be able to solve. Just saying something like "understand Hadoop" is not compelling. Instead, I led with "Design distributed systems that manage big data using Hadoop and related technologies." Use verbs that convey action; I used words like "analyze," "query", "design", "choose," and "create" while coming up with this list.

From looking at a real landing page, we know that only the top 6 or so skills you list will actually appear above the fold of the course landing page. It's critical to get the top keywords you care about in those first six slots.

You might remember that "big data", "Hadoop", and "Spark" were the top 3 keywords for this particular topic, and I've worked them into those top 6 skills for that reason.

As with crafting a title, there's more to it than just keyword stuffing. You also want to convey the story of how your course will allow your students to do things they couldn't do before. Just listing off the topics your course covers may make search engines happy, however it won't make your potential students excited when they read them.

This is really the #1 non-obvious thing you can do to help out a course. Most instructors don't give this section of the "target student" tab the attention it deserves, because it's sort of presented as just an exercise to think through who your target student is. In reality, what you type in here makes up half of your course landing page! It's hugely important to make it compelling, and to work in the keywords you care about.

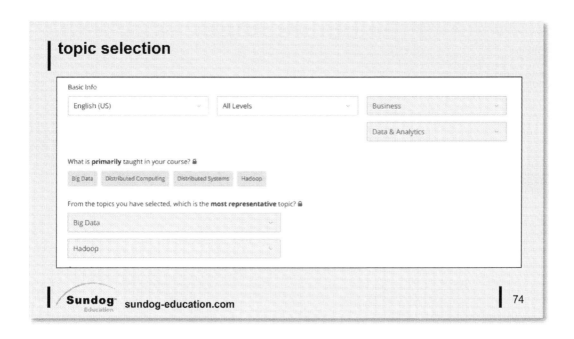

We talked about topic selection at length earlier, but it's worth re-iterating that the actual category and sub-category deserves careful attention if there is more than one combination that fits your course. I chose the Business category and "Data & Analytics" sub-category, because I determined that particular sub-category was less competitive.

You can also select individual topics that are relevant to your course, as well as the most relevant topic. You will of course want to choose the topics with the highest search volume that you discovered while using the Marketplace Insights tool to refine your choice of keywords, but while still being honest. Don't tag yourself with topics that aren't actually the primary focus of your course. If more than one topic applies to your course, pick the one that's searched for more often.

> **Course Description Example**
>
> **B** *I* ≡ ≡
>
> The world of **Hadoop** and **"Big Data"** can be intimidating - hundreds of different technologies with cryptic names form the Hadoop ecosystem. With this Hadoop tutorial, you'll not only understand what those systems are and how they fit together - but you'll go hands-on and learn how to use them to solve real business problems!
>
> Learn and master the most popular big data technologies in this comprehensive course, taught by a former engineer and senior manager from **Amazon** and **IMDb**. We'll go way beyond Hadoop itself, and dive into all sorts of distributed systems you may need to integrate with.
>
> - Install and work with a real Hadoop installation right on your desktop with **Hortonworks** (now part of Cloudera) and the **Ambari** UI
> - Manage big data on a cluster with **HDFS** and **MapReduce**
> - Write programs to analyze data on Hadoop with **Pig** and **Spark**
> - Store and query your data with **Sqoop**, **Hive**, **MySQL**, **HBase**, **Cassandra**, **MongoDB**, **Drill**, **Phoenix**, and **Presto**
> - **Design real-world systems** using the Hadoop ecosystem
> - Learn how your cluster is managed with **YARN**, **Mesos**, **Zookeeper**, **Oozie**, **Zeppelin**, and **Hue**
> - Handle streaming data in real time with **Kafka**, **Flume**, **Spark Streaming**, **Flink**, and **Storm**
>
> Understanding Hadoop is a highly valuable skill for anyone working at companies with large amounts of data.
>
> Almost every large company you might want to work at uses Hadoop in some way, including Amazon, Ebay, Facebook, Google, LinkedIn, IBM, Spotify, Twitter, and Yahoo! And it's not just technology companies that need Hadoop; even the New York Times uses Hadoop for processing images.
>
> Knowing how to wrangle "big data" is an incredibly valuable skill for today's top tech employers. Don't be left behind - **enroll now!**

It's interesting that the course description isn't actually above the fold on your course landing page. Students have to look for it to find it. It's still important from an SEO standpoint. You'll notice that I worked in my top two keywords right at the top: "Hadoop" and "Big Data," and both are even in boldface. Other keywords I want to rank for are also included, also in bold.

Structurally, all of my course descriptions follow a similar format. First, I start with a description of the problem my course solves for my students. In this case, it's eliminating confusion over the huge array of oddly named technologies in the world of big data.

Then, I validate myself as an instructor. Why should you want to learn from me? What are my qualifications? Udemy courses and instructors are not accredited in any way, so it's up to you to convince students that you're an expert in what you're teaching, and that you're qualified to teach it.

Next up is a bullet list of the main topics and technologies the course will cover. As with the "what will I learn?" section, you want to write these with the actions and capabilities your course will enable, and not just a laundry list of topics. Instead of just listing "HDFS and MapReduce," I said "Manage big data on a cluster with HDFS and MapReduce."

In the next couple of paragraphs, I convey why the knowledge I'm offering is valuable. Why should a student care about it? What's in it for them? You really need to think about what your students are looking for. What they're REALLY looking for. They're not really looking to learn some specific technology or something; they want to learn that technology for a reason. I've learned over time that my own students are usually trying to find a better-paying job than what they have today, by learning a hot technical skill at a low price.

I talk about the big-name employers that use the technologies I'm teaching, and what sorts of employers might value the knowledge I'm conveying. I don't make any promises I can't keep about them actually getting a job, I just state how these skills are relevant to today's job market.

Your students might be after something totally different. Maybe you teach a course on painting. Are students really looking to understand how to use a fan brush effectively? No; they just want to make paintings they can be proud of and have a sense of accomplishment after creating them. Or maybe they use painting as a way to relax and unplug a bit from the real world. Those might both be things you try to convey in your course description.

After this I focus on the value the student will receive from the course. Look at all the topics it covers! Look at how much content you're getting for your $10! Look at all the hands-on practice and experience this course will give you! You have to convey how your course delivers more value than the ones you're competing against here. If it doesn't, well, you need to go add some more content to it!

It talks a bit about who this course is for, and the pre-requisite knowledge they must have to be successful. I also talk about who the course isn't for; many poor reviews just arise from a poor match between student and course. Some students are looking for a specific skill level, or a specific aspect of your topic that you may or may not focus on. It's best to just be up front about who won't be satisfied with your course, because you don't want those students enrolling and leaving a bad review.

There is also another description of what this course will enable for the student. "You'll walk away from this course with a real, deep understanding of Hadoop and its associated distributed systems, and you can apply Hadoop to real-world problems." That's ultimately the value this course delivers to the student, and that's a good note to end on.

If you have any student testimonials or reviews that talk about the results they achieved by taking your course – like landing a new job, or building something at work – that's great to include as well. It's also a good idea to end with a "call to action," such as "what are you waiting for? Enroll now!"

To recap, a good course description:

- Includes your top keywords

- Conveys the new capabilities your course delivers to students

- Establishes your credentials to teach the topic

- Lists the main skills your course delivers, phrased as actions

- Conveys why students should care about learning your topic

- Addresses what students are looking for by learning your topic

- Establishes who the course is for, and who it isn't for

- Includes student testimonials speaking to the results they achieved

- Ends with a call to action to enroll in your course

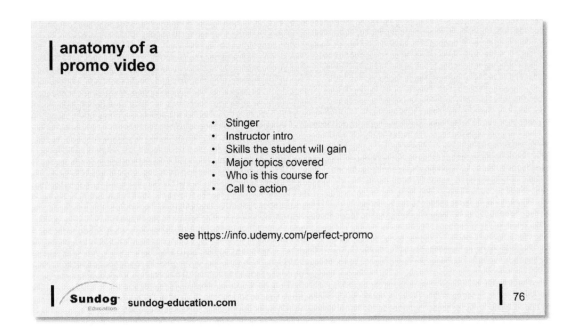

Another thing that's really prominent on your course landing page is the course preview, which leads students to your course's promotional video if they click on it. I've found that it's worth your time to make your promo videos as good as they can be.

Even a modest improvement in production quality can boost your conversion rates significantly, so it's an effort that can pay off quickly. Students are trying to bargain-hunt on Udemy, finding pro-quality content at a low price. If your promo video reflects professional production standards, they'll gravitate toward your course and away from the courses that don't.

Many instructors don't create a promo video at all, and many of those who do just film themselves talking in some cluttered environment for several minutes. It's not too hard to make your course stand out with a well-produced promo video.

As an example, I updated the promo video for my second most-popular course on data science recently, and immediately saw my conversion rate jump from around 4% to over 5%. Not only does that increased conversion rate translate into more course sales, it's also a signal to Udemy's algorithms that students like what they see on your landing page – which will cause Udemy to promote your course more aggressively, leading to even more sales. One month after updating the promo video, my data science course became my new best-selling course, by a fairly large margin. And it's not as if the promo video it replaced was all that bad, either.

Structurally, you should keep your promo video under 2 minutes, as students don't have much of an attention span while they're shopping. Udemy offers a well-researched recipe for how to structure your promo video at https://info.udemy.com/perfect-promo, and I don't have a lot to add to their recommendations. I've followed this recipe, and it has worked well. Promo videos are the one thing you should always script out, word for word, ahead of time, since every word does count.

To summarize, start with a little 5-second "stinger," or intro clip that displays your course title and who you are. The idea is to grab the student's attention during those first few seconds and draw them in; a brief bit of music can be useful for this. You can license short music clips at sites such as sounddogs.com; just search for "stinger" or "intro" and browse until you hear something you like. Expect to pay around $20 to license a few seconds of music for this intro.

Then, introduce yourself and briefly summarize your qualifications. Next, cover the skills the student will gain – what will they be able to do after finishing your course that they couldn't do before? Always remember to write your script with the student's viewpoint in mind. What problem are you solving for them? Speak to that, not why you as an instructor think your course is great.

Briefly summarize the major topics your course will cover, again keeping in mind which topics are the most important to your students based on your keyword research. This is a good chance to work in some motion graphics and overlays to maintain visual interest in the video – you want to break up the image of your talking head a bit. Sped-up clips of relevant screencast lectures in your course are good to include as well.

Next talk about the type of person the course is for. You want the students who will benefit the most from your course to think "yeah, that's me!" when you describe that ideal student. So again, script this with the student's viewpoint in mind.

Finally, wrap up with a call to action, like "check out the preview videos and hit the enroll button," or "with Udemy's money-back guarantee there's nothing to lose, and everything to gain – sign up now!"

Although it's only a couple of minutes of video, you should plan to spend an entire day to produce your promo video. You really need to be at your best when making it.

As an example, this is the promo video I talked about earlier that made my #2 course into my #1 course within the space of a month. If you're not viewing this in video form, you can search Udemy for my data science course and see it on its landing page.

When you do watch it, take note of the sections recommended by Udemy's recipe: the stinger, instructor intro, skills the course delivers, major topics covered, who the course is for, and the closing call to action.

From an editing standpoint, notice how visual interest is maintained using motion, moving my image around in the frame, and interspersing clips from the course, stock footage, and motion graphics to maintain the student's attention.

I can't take credit for this myself – I actually paid a professional video editor to put this together, using the original green-screen footage I recorded for my original take at the promo video.

That sort of investment will only make sense for a top-selling course, but the idea here is to give you something good to look at, and hopefully give you some inspiration and new ideas from it.

Watching a professionally-produced promo video is inspiring and can give you some new ideas. I want to also show you what you can achieve as an amateur, just editing it yourself. This is a promo video for my course on Spark Streaming, and again, if you're not viewing this in video form, you can search for it on Udemy and just watch it there.

It's not up to the production standards of the previous video, however it follows Udemy's recipe for a perfect promo video, and is still better than most promo videos. It too had a very measurable impact on the course's conversion rate, though it only cost me some time to re-record the talking head segments and edit it using Camtasia. Producing something of this quality is an achievable goal just using the equipment and techniques I've already introduced you to.

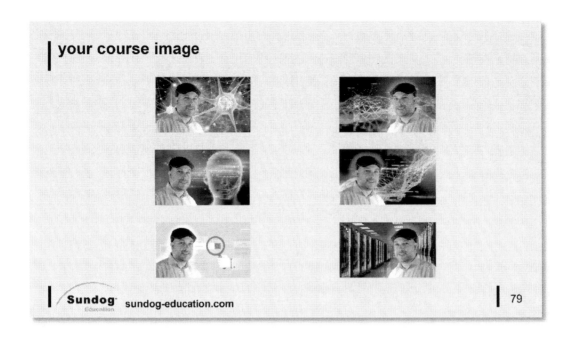

Another little thing that can have a surprisingly large impact on sales is the quality of your course image. While students are browsing search results, your course title and this image are the main things they are going to see. If your image catches their attention and draws their eye to your title, then your course will sell all that much more.

Udemy offers a free course image design service, but if you're serious about succeeding on Udemy, I don't recommend using it. Your image will end up looking like everyone else's, and your goal is to stand out. It's worth an hour or two of your time to create your own course image that students will see as different and compelling.

Here are some examples of my course images. First of all, remember Udemy's policies – you're not allowed to have text in your image, unless it's part of a logo. This is because Udemy may localize your course into other languages, and you don't want English-language text in an image for a course marketed at, say, Japanese-speaking students.

A little mind-hack that I use is the knowledge that people's attention is drawn to human faces. So, I include an image of my face on all of my course images. Not only does it grab the student's attention, it also creates a consistent branding with all of my courses, which is kind of nice. Try to look as warm and inviting as you can manage if you also use a photo of yourself in your image.

It's not strictly necessary to use a headshot in your course image if you're not comfortable with doing so; the main thing is to create an image that's different enough from the generic ones that come from Udemy's free image service to catch the eye. Try searching Udemy for the topic you're teaching, and look at the course images you'll be competing with. How can you produce something different and more eye-catching than what is currently on the first page of search results for your topic?

The mechanics of producing the images above are straightforward. I took a headshot of myself against a green screen, and removed the background to make it transparent. I'm just using that same headshot over and over, in some cases flipped horizontally if I want to be on a different side of the image. I'm just using a free image editor called Paint.NET for all of this.

I start by creating a canvas of 750x422 resolution, which is the size Udemy requires. I'll then find a relevant background image that I've licensed from iStockPhoto.com, and scale it down to fit into a background layer on this image.

Next I'll create a new layer, and paste in my headshot with a transparent background. Finally, I'll paint a soft, semi-transparent white glow around the edges of my headshot in the background layer, to help my image pop out from the background image.

When students are searching for a course, they'll be drawn to the human faces they see – and when they see mine, they'll also see a professionally produced background image that I licensed for just a few dollars, again signaling to them that this course is higher-quality than most.

It's not hard to create an image for your course that stands out in a good way, and it's absolutely time well spent.

exercise: optimize your course landing page

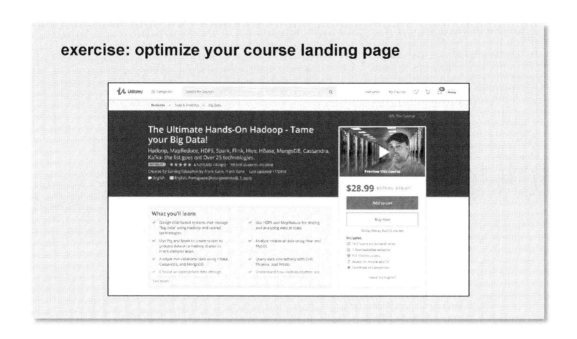

While it's fresh in your head, apply what you've learned! If you already have a course on Udemy, edit its landing page to improve its SEO. Tweak your title and subtitle; update your course image; maybe even update your promo video. Look critically at the "What you'll learn" section, and think about how you can make it more compelling. Little changes here can go a long way.

If you're making your first course, fill your landing page details and target student information, with what we've just covered in mind.

CHAPTER 8 – Pre-Launch Planning

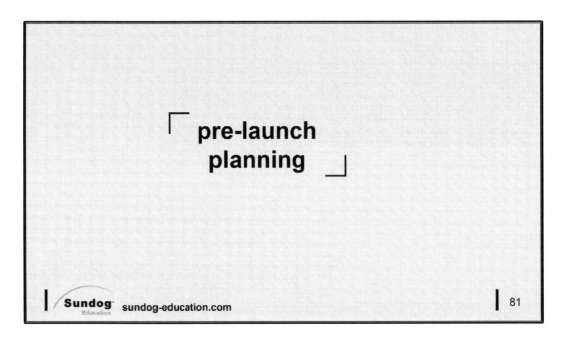

Before you publish your course, it pays to think about how you can maintain a connection with the students who enroll in it. Udemy won't give you any personal information about your students, so if you want the ability to reach them through your own mailing list or through social media, you need to entice them into providing that personal information voluntarily.

Doing this in a way that's within Udemy's policies requires some care, so let's talk about ways of building direct communication lines with your students that won't land you in trouble with Udemy's trust and safety team.

We'll also discuss a few other considerations you need to address before you publish your course, such as preventing piracy and keeping your content safe, and deciding on a price for your course. In the end of this section, you'll develop a pre-launch checklist for your course to make sure you don't forget anything important.

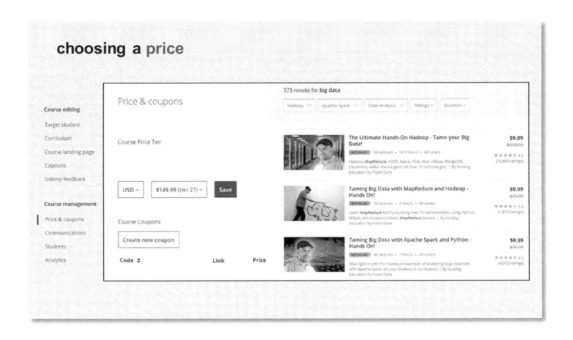

Something that new instructors find confusing is how to set the right price for your course.

The reality is: it doesn't really matter what your list price is set to. Almost every sale you make will be from a fixed-price promotion Udemy is running between $10 and $15 USD. On the right, you can see that three of my courses come up if I search for "big data," and the price you see is $9.99 for all of them. My list price is shown underneath the $9.99 with a strikethrough, but it's the $9.99 that your eye is drawn to.

You might say that psychologically, the bigger the perceived discount, the better – and so you should always price your courses as high as possible. Udemy advises pricing your courses in line with the value they deliver.

My oldest course is shown as the second result here, and as it's only 5 hours and not really up to my current standards, I've priced it as $79.99. But the top result is my flagship course that has almost 15 hours of content, and it's priced at $179.99. I think about what I would actually feel comfortable selling the course at, if Udemy's massive scale weren't part of the equation. Udemy is always experimenting with different pricing strategies, so you want to make sure your list price at least makes sense if they start to move more toward percentage-based discounts, or even full-price sales, which does happen rarely.

It's a good idea to look at the competing courses in your topic, and choose a list price that's competitive given the amount of content you are offering. Udemy students are extremely price-conscious, so you need to find a balance where the price is low enough to be competitive if Udemy isn't running a promotion, however high enough so that the perceived discount on $10 fixed-price sales looks like a great value as well. I think most students know that list prices are currently meaningless on Udemy, you just don't want to be caught off-guard if that changes someday.

So, pick a list price that's in line with the amount of content your course offers, and in line with the list prices of competing courses in your topic.

preventing piracy

- Don't respond to beggars
- Don't give out lots of free coupons
- Don't enable video downloads
- Make your course depend on other stuff
- Watermark your videos
- Be careful where you publish
- Don't give out your raw slides
- udemy.pirashield.com

Although people like to debate just how much harm piracy does, it's still prudent to take steps to protect the content of your course. There are few things more frustrating than finding someone who is offering all of your course videos for free when you worked so hard to produce them, or even worse, selling them as their own work.

The even bigger impact is when a pirate site comes up before Udemy in search results when people are looking for your course on Google. Unfortunately, word has gotten out that there is money in the world of online courses, and it's attracted a lot of unsavory characters. Some have convinced themselves that "knowledge is free" and they are somehow righting the evil of instructors expecting $10 for a course they spent months creating. I'll stop ranting now.

The main thing is to remain vigilant. You can't assume that everyone who contacts you has good intentions.

A very common scheme is to go around begging instructors for free coupons to their paid courses, claiming some sort of tragedy that prevents them from paying even $10 for it. They will hoard all of these courses that they got for free, and then sell their Udemy account that contains thousands of dollars' worth of courses for a handsome profit.

If someone you don't know sends you a direct message begging for a free coupon, just ignore it. Don't even respond to say no, because then there's a chance they'll choose to retaliate somehow.

Free coupons also give people a chance to steal all of your course's content without paying a penny, and post it to torrent sites or sell it as their own. I do not recommend giving out free coupons under any circumstances, unless it's to someone you know and trust.

I also don't enable downloads of my video lectures. Yes, there are tools on the black market that can download all of a course's videos even if you don't enable downloads – but why make it easier for pirates?

If a legitimate student wants to view your lectures while offline, the Udemy mobile app will allow them to do so, in a more secure manner. If someone contacts you begging you to enable downloads with some story about how bad the Internet is in their country, there's a good chance you're being scammed. Again, ignore the message.

In reality, there's nothing you can do to prevent piracy entirely. If a pirate wants to steal your content badly enough, there are ways for them to do it with enough effort. You also need to figure out how to make that stolen content as worthless as possible.

One way is to make sure your course depends on materials other than just the lecture videos. If your videos instruct students to download sample code or exercises from the resources in Udemy, someone who stole your course just might do the right thing and actually buy it in order to gain access to those materials needed to actually take the course.

To protect against people selling your content as their own, include a watermark on all of your slides and videos. You can see my slides all have a Sundog Education logo and URL at the bottom. This is within Udemy's policies, and it makes it very difficult for someone else to present my videos as their own work.

Also, be careful where you publish your courses. Udemy at least has some measures to discourage piracy in place, but smaller online education platforms might just offer up raw links to MP4 files to their students. With every platform you publish to outside of Udemy, you're taking a risk that students will steal your content from that platform. Most of the pirated copies I see of my own content can be traced back to publishers who aren't Udemy.

Many students expect a copy of your course slides. You're under no obligation to provide those; it's not part of the deal. Giving students your raw PowerPoint slides just makes it very easy for them take your content, modify it, and present it as their own.

If you do offer your slides to students, at least export them in PDF form to make them a little bit harder to edit, and make sure your slides are watermarked with your name or logo.

Finally, if you do encounter a copy of your course on a pirate site, Udemy can help. Visit udemy.pirashield.com, and you'll be directed to LinkBusters, which is a company Udemy has contracted with to file DMCA takedown requests on your behalf.

If you find a link to your pirated course, just copy those links into the form at LinkBusters, and they'll file takedown requests. While many pirate sites ignore takedown requests, at a minimum they can get Google to blacklist those links to your pirated content, so you won't be competing with pirate sites in Google search results.

Sometimes several links are involved in pirated content – be sure to report not only the pirate site itself, but also the link to the site that's actually hosting your pirated course which might be someplace like CloudFlare or something. Even if the pirate site won't take down your content, the site that's hosting it might.

A feature in Udemy that might sound appealing is the automatic course messages you can send to students upon enrollment and upon completion of your course. You can set these up under the "communications" section of your course editing screen, under the "course messages" tab.

The idea of the welcome message when a student enrolls is to encourage them to start your course. A lot of students buy courses, and then never actually take them. Seems like a good idea, and when you're just starting and need to get as many reviews as you can, it's probably worth using this feature to try and get new students engaged with your course and ultimately writing the reviews you need to get your course off the ground.

Once you're established, those welcome messages can do more harm than good. The problem is it establishes a direct line of communication between you and the student. When that student has a question about the course, they're going to be more inclined to message you directly about it than to use Udemy's Q&A feature. This make it impossible to outsource Q&A support to a teaching assistant, and it also prevents other students from seeing and benefiting from your answer to the question. You end up being on-call to students all the time, answering the same questions over and over again.

That's why I've left the welcome message blank on my courses. If students have a question, I want them to use the Q&A feature, not a direct message in reply to the welcome message Udemy's robots sent to them.

Sending congratulations messages upon course completion is a good idea, however. You want to reinforce the value the student received from your course, and close with a call to action for them to leave a review or update the one they wrote earlier. You can't explicitly ask for a positive review, but presumably if they made it all the way through the course, they liked it. And a written review from someone who completed your course counts for a LOT in Udemy's review score algorithm.

Students who finish your course are unfortunately few and far between, so the direct message traffic you'll get in response to congratulations messages will be low. They're usually just thanking you for making a good course, which are the messages we like to see!

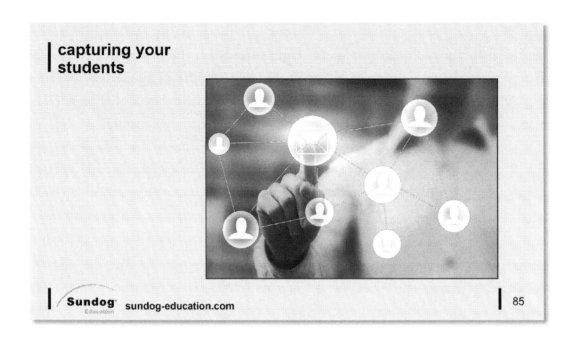

One downside to using platforms such as Udemy, is that Udemy owns the student relationship, not you. There is no way for you to contact students outside of the Udemy platform, no way for you to get their email addresses, and any communication you have with students has to be through Udemy's tools and following Udemy's strict rules about what you're allowed to promote to them, and when. It's not that Udemy is evil – they're just trying to protect their students from incessant spam from instructors, within reason. If you want to be able to leverage the relationship you build with your students on Udemy, you need to find ways to encourage them to provide their contact information to you voluntarily.

That way, even if you decide to leave the Udemy platform at some point in the future, you'll still have an audience you can market your future offerings to. Let's discuss a few ways in which you can motivate students to connect with you outside of Udemy's walls, that are within the bounds of Udemy's policies.

One trick is to host the materials or setup instructions for your course on your own website, and direct your students to that site early on in your course. Udemy is OK with this, provided that the page you are sending them to is primarily for providing educational content, and you are not forcing students to provide any personal information to access it.

It's OK to have a button, like I do, that offers a lead magnet of a free course or something in exchange for signing up for your mailing list, or to have links to your social media presence so they can follow you there. It just has to be unobtrusive – you can't have a big pop-up that students have to dismiss before they can get to the educational content they came for.

In the course materials page, the materials they need are in the main column, but opportunities to connect and see my other courses are in the right-hand column.

This is a somewhat sneaky way to capture students and sell them on your other courses, however as they are free to do so or not voluntarily, Udemy is OK with this sort of thing.

Building up a mailing list of your own can be a powerful marketing tool, especially if you plan to offer products or services outside of the Udemy platform to your Udemy students.

I use MailChimp as my mailing list platform, and that "Sign Up for my Free Course" button redirects to a MailChimp signup form, which kicks off an automated email campaign that sends them a link to that course and some follow-up messages over time.

Another benefit of hosting your own materials is that it makes your course more portable to other platforms. If your setup video just directs students to your own website instead of materials hosted on a specific online learning platform, then you can re-use the same lecture videos on platforms other than Udemy with basically zero work.

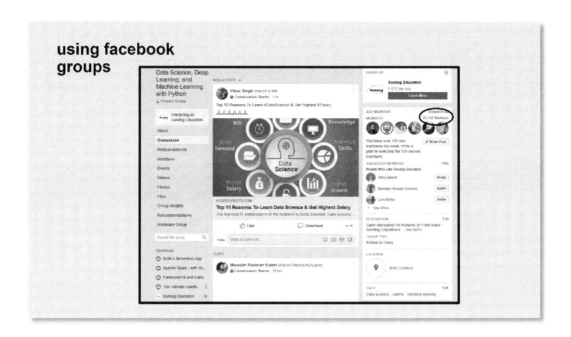

Udemy is also totally OK with directing students to a social media group associated with your course that you control. On my course materials page, and within the course itself, I invite students to join a Facebook Group for that course. Udemy asks that your group is primarily educational in nature; you can't just keep spamming it with promotions to your other courses – it has to provide real educational value first and foremost.

I think of it as a way for students to collaborate with each other and get help on problems outside the scope of the course itself, and it's also an insurance policy in case Udemy gets acquired or something and takes their student list with them. If that were to happen, at least I can reach those students through Facebook.

In this one group, I've amassed over 43,000 members who are interested in the topic I teach. That might come in handy someday.

However, the value of Facebook Groups, and Facebook in general, is relatively small. People don't come to Facebook to buy things, so even if you do try to sell these people something, they're very unlikely to act on it. It depends a lot on your audience, too – some segments are easier to sell to than others.

Let me point out a mistake I made in setting this particular group, so you can learn from it. I just used the title of my course, "Data Science, Deep Learning, and Machine Learning with Python" as the name of the group. And even though it is a closed group, it ended up attracting a large number of people – mostly from India, for some reason – who just wanted to join a group on that subject area, but have never even heard of my course, much less enrolled in it.

There's a lot of discussion of competing courses on other platforms in this group, because most people in it don't even know the group is for my course. This has made the moderation of the group difficult; its size has attracted a lot of spam, scammers, and trolls that need to be dealt with on a daily basis, and frankly moderating a large Facebook group is a soul-crushing job.

I ended up hiring someone to do it for me, so really, I'm losing money on this group. If I could do it over again, I'd put "Sundog Education" in the group name to make it more obvious that it's not just a general group for anyone interested in data science.

So, if you create a Facebook Group for your course – make sure the name makes it clear that it's only for your students. I'm not sure it's something I'd necessarily recommend setting up for new instructors, but some instructors report more success using Facebook Groups than I've personally seen. It doesn't cost anything to give it a try at least.

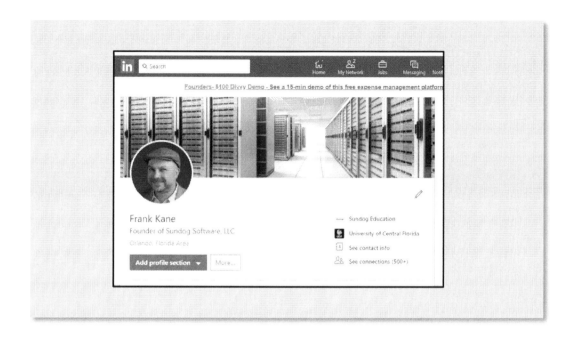

Something really easy, is to just have a presence on LinkedIn. I'm not entirely sure how, but a large number of students track me down on LinkedIn and connect with me there. I just checked and I've amassed over 4,000 connections, and the vast majority of them are students. That's 4,000 students that I can message and communicate with however I wish, since they chose to connect with me outside of the class. When I launch a new course, I announce it on LinkedIn, and quite a few of those people will enroll just from seeing it there. Writing articles on LinkedIn is also a good way to maintain those student relationships. Don't just accept every connection request you see, though. There are a lot of people trying to sell services to you, so at least take a quick look at the job title of the people who are trying to connect to make sure they are in an industry related to what you teach. Remember you can include your social media links within your Udemy profile as well, to make it even easier for students to find you on LinkedIn, Twitter, Facebook, YouTube, or your own site.

Now that we've covered all the little tips and tricks associated with creating the content for your course, and working on ways to capture student contact information within Udemy's policies, let's talk about the final steps involved with actually publishing your course.

Once you've finished recording and editing your videos, and you're happy with your course landing page from an SEO standpoint, you're just about ready to hit the "submit for review" button – and things can move quickly once that happens!

You need to be ready to start promoting your new course the moment it hits the marketplace, and preparing a plan and the materials you need ahead of time will ensure it goes smoothly.

your pre-launch checklist

- ☐ Double-check curriculum and CLP
- ☐ Select free preview lectures
- ☐ Prepare YouTube videos
- ☐ Prepare Udemy promo announcement
- ☐ Prepare mailing list announcement
- ☐ Prepare social media announcements
- ☐ Prepare blog posts
- ☐ Hit the submit button!

I like to prepare a little checklist just before launching a new course, to make sure I don't forget anything important. There are lots of little things that are easy to overlook!

Here's what my own list usually looks like.

Some of these steps might not apply to you, so let's talk through each one so you can work on creating your own pre-launch success, and make sure your course launch goes as smoothly as possible.

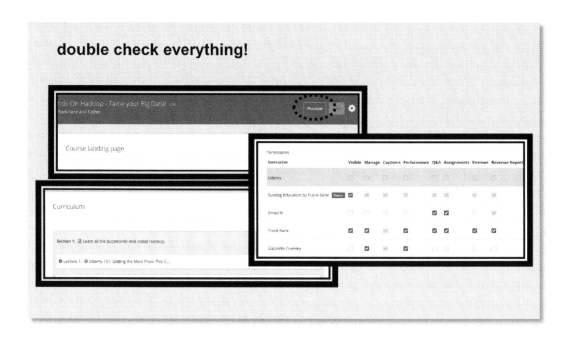

The first step is to double-check all of your content and settings prior to submitting the course for review to Udemy.

Your course landing page is the first thing your potential new students will see, so you want to make sure you didn't forget anything there. From your landing page area on your course editing screen, there's a preview button that lets you view your landing page as a student will see it.

Try to look at it through a student's eyes. Does it look professionally produced? Does it speak to the benefit the course will give the student? Are your promo video and course image looking as good as they can?

When you're this close to finishing a big project like this, you probably don't want to deal with feedback and new things you need to fix – but it would be a really good idea to have someone else take a look at your landing page and tell you what is and isn't compelling before you publish it. Udemy will only give your new course increased exposure for a limited amount of time, so it's important that it makes a good initial impression upon launch. This is especially important if English is not your native language; grammatical errors on your landing page will be a real turn-off for prospective students, and that's an entirely preventable problem if you just ask someone to proofread it for you.

You'll also want to double-check your curriculum items. It's very easy to accidentally drag and drop a lecture into the wrong section, or into the wrong position within a section.

Are any lectures missing? Did you remember to enter descriptions for each lecture? Are there any resource attachments that you mention in the lectures that you forgot to attach?

You want to be the one to catch those kinds of mistakes, not your first students. The reviews of those early students can really make or break your course, so try to make their experience as error-free as possible.

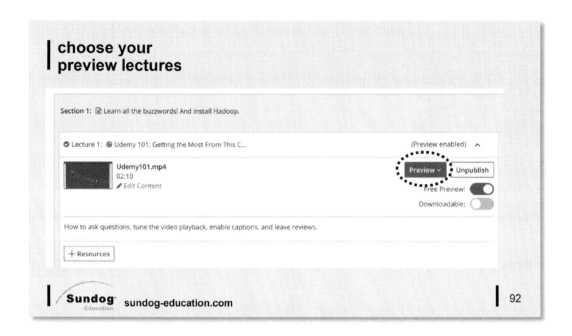

Don't forget to check your course settings as well. You can get here through the gear icon on your course editing screen, and it's an easy thing to forget.

If you have any co-instructors or assistants, did you remember to add them to the course, and set up any revenue split you agreed upon?

It would sure create a mess if you agreed to split the revenue with someone, and then started selling courses before you remembered to set that split-up in your course settings.

Don't forget to select which lectures you'll enable as free preview lectures. When a student is previewing your course, they will be able to watch the set of lectures you're enabled "free preview" on, prior to enrolling.

I recommend marking your very best, most visually compelling lectures for free preview. It may seem counter-intuitive to give away your best content, it's just that students want to see that the quality of your course is not limited to the promo video before they purchase.

Generally, I pick the best video from each section of my course, and mark it as a "Free Preview" lecture. Try to capture both the best slide-based lectures, and the best hands-on activities in the course. Just be careful not to enable free preview on any content that you have a good reason to restrict to paid students, such as lectures that direct students to course materials or services that you don't want to give away for free. Udemy policies also prohibit you from marking your final "Bonus Lecture" as a free preview, so resist the temptation to do that as well.

prepare YouTube videos

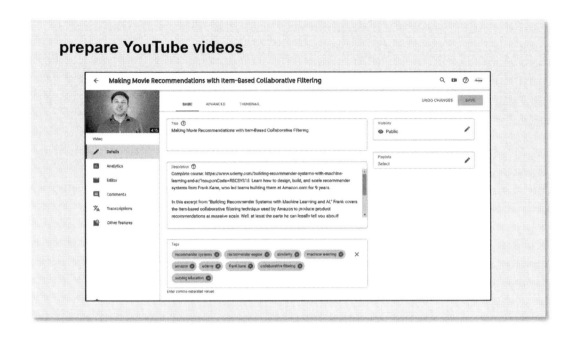

Using YouTube as a marketing tool isn't as effective as it once was; people on YouTube are generally only interested in free content. You can still drive a few sales this way, so there's no good reason not to set up a YouTube channel and upload your preview videos there as well.

Prior to launching your course, you can upload the videos and draft the title, description, and tags for the preview videos you want to put on YouTube. You're going to need an actual coupon link to your course to include in the description however, and you won't have that until your course is live on the Udemy marketplace. So, don't publish your YouTube videos just yet – just focus on getting them ready to publish quickly after you've launched, and can paste in a coupon code that will allow you to track enrollments that came from your YouTube videos.

As with your free preview lectures on Udemy, you'll want to put some of your best content on YouTube as well. Just don't put all of it there; Udemy does not allow you to offer an entire course for free on YouTube if you're charging for it on Udemy. The lectures you want to select for YouTube might be different from the free lectures you selected on Udemy, however. The videos that do well on YouTube are the ones that solve a specific problem someone is searching for on YouTube. Choose videos that can largely stand on their own, and teach some specific skill people are actively looking to learn.

The most popular video on my own channel is simply titled "Elasticsearch Architecture" – it's a self-contained lecture that explains how a complex piece of technology works under the hood, and apparently 22,000 people wanted to know that badly enough to actually watch that video.

Other types of videos that do well include "FAQ" videos related to your topic, videos similar to the top videos you see in YouTube when you search for your topic, and longer videos. YouTube decides which videos to promote based on how many minutes viewers spend watching them, so the longer your video, the better – as long as you can hold the viewer's attention for the entire time! Videos with the word "tutorial" in the title tend to do well, as well as "top 10" lists, or videos on the latest emerging trends in your field.

If you have the time, it might help to add a really short intro to your video explaining that it's an excerpt from a larger course (see the link in the description!) and a short call to action at the end, reminding the viewer to check out the link to your course in the description.

Most YouTube viewers will decide whether to keep watching your video after just seeing the first 5 seconds of it, so if you do add an intro, make sure you look excited and energetic, yet humble. Viewers on YouTube want to watch people they can relate to.

The first thing in your video description should be that link to your course, and it will have to be a placeholder until your course is actually published. Don't skimp on your description; the longer it is, and the more relevant keywords it contains, the more likely your video is to get surfaced. You want to aim for like a thousand words here.

Don't forget to add relevant tags to your video – the more, the better.

You can put as much or as little effort into YouTube videos to promote your course as you want, but it's a good idea to get most of it out of the way before you launch your course.

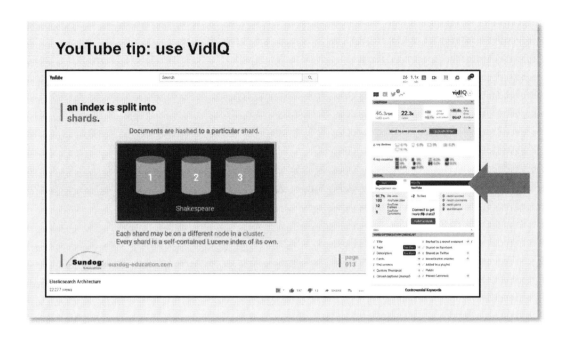

As you can probably gather, there's a whole science to search engine optimization on YouTube, with its own set of tricks. If you're not an expert YouTube marketer, or even if you are, there's a nice browser extension called VidIQ that can help you optimize your YouTube channel.

Once you install it, it will show a bunch of stats next to any of your videos that showcase how you're doing from an SEO standpoint. It will give you specific recommendations, like your title is too long, or you need more tags on your videos. All you have to do is follow its advice as best you can.

VidIQ can also help you research keywords and come up with the best titles for your YouTube videos. All you have to do is search for something in YouTube, and it will tell you how many people are searching for that keyword, and related search terms that you might want to consider instead.

For example, I searched for "Hadoop" on YouTube (and two of my own videos appeared! Yay!) On the right, you can see that 267,000 people per month are searching for "Hadoop," and I can see how that compares to other search terms, and how competitive this keyword is. It also shows me the top related queries, so I know a lot of people are specifically searching for "Hadoop tutorial."

It's no coincidence that the title of my own video is titled "Hadoop Tutorial for Beginners"! That's exactly how I arrived at that title.

Another top result is titled "What is Hadoop?" – and that's another good strategy; phrasing your title in the form of a question that people might be typing into YouTube's search bar.

Don't try and overthink this too much, though. The truth is that some videos I uploaded into YouTube before I knew any of these tricks are doing better than my newer ones that try to follow all of these best practices. It's hard to know what will take off and what won't on YouTube. There's certainly a degree of luck to it.

If this isn't your first course, the most powerful tool you have to promote your new course is Udemy's promotional announcements feature. It allows you to send an email to all of your existing students announcing a special offer for your new course – well, at least all of the existing students who haven't opted out of Udemy's emails.

This is hugely important, because your existing students include your biggest fans. These are the people who are both most likely to enroll in your new course, and to leave a positive review if they do enroll in it. Those early enrollments, and early reviews, can make or break a new course. Without a promo announcement, you might have to wait a long time for your first honest review to come in, and it's going to be hard to attract new students on a course that has no reviews and few enrollments.

The promo announcement is the tool you need to jump-start that process. That early surge of enrollments from your existing fans also gives your course a really high conversion rate, which is a signal to Udemy's algorithms to start promoting your new course more heavily on the platform.

When you're launching your very first course, you don't have any existing students to send a promotional announcement to, and that's why success is so hard to come by on your first course. Once you've amassed a student base, launching subsequent courses becomes a whole lot easier, because they are now an audience you can market to.

You create a promotional announcement by using the "create a new…" button in your instructor dashboard – however you can't draft an announcement and save it to send for later. You'll want to draft the text of your promotional announcement in Word or Google Docs or something ahead of time, so you can just copy and paste it in when your course launches and you're ready to actually launch the announcement for it.

How do you craft an effective promo announcement? Well, a lot of the same tips apply from when you wrote your course description. The main thing is to speak to the problem you're solving for students, and not just about how great your course is.

Start with a compelling title so people will open your announcement; for a new course, start with the phrase "New course!" as that will tell students that this is something special they should act on.

Lead off with the value your course will deliver – in this case, it's teaching valuable algorithms that can translate into careers at some highly desirable employers. Link to your course early and often – and again, you'll need to leave a placeholder for this, since you won't have actual coupon links until after your course is published.

After that, I touch on the main skills the course teaches, the scope of the course, and the value for the money it offers. I close with a final call to action to enroll, using a coupon link.

You kind of have to know your audience, as well. Many email marketers will recommend using hard-sell techniques such as limited time offers to create a sense of urgency. But I think those sorts of techniques insult the intelligence of my students, and make me come across as a salesman instead of as a teacher. There's a line I try not to cross there. If you're teaching multi-level marketing or something, your students might expect that sort of approach!

You have to decide just how "sales-y" you're willing to be, and how much of that approach your existing students will tolerate.

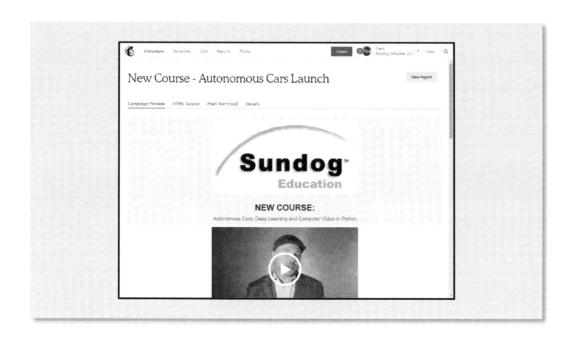

If you have a mailing list, promoting new courses to it is kind of the whole reason to have one! People who have chosen to subscribe to your announcements want to hear about your new course more than anyone.

I use mailchimp.com for my email platform. It makes it easy to integrate a signup form on my website, and to send bulk mail in a way that probably won't be filtered as spam. It also provides an easy mechanism for people to opt out of your emails, which is really important now for legal reasons. Don't even consider managing your own email list and just sending an email to everyone using Gmail or something. That's a great way to make sure your personal emails become undeliverable, and to find yourself in legal hot water for not adhering to the various spam-related laws around the globe.

MailChimp also allows you to draft emails ahead of time, which means you can get this announcement almost ready to send as soon as your course launches. You can use pretty much the same copy you used for your Udemy promotional announcement, but you're not limited by what's allowed by Udemy. Links to your own websites, and inclusion of your course promo video and not just an image, are fair game when you're sending your own emails on your own terms.

So, get this announcement set up ahead of time, and just add in the coupon links to your course once it launches, then schedule its delivery. Platforms such as MailChimp have a nice feature that will automatically send your email at the times most likely to be read by your students, so you don't have to guess about it.

If you don't have a mailing list – that's OK. We already discussed putting a signup link on your course materials pages on your website, and we'll talk about full-blown sales funnels a little later in the course. Both are effective means of building up a mailing list of your own.

Some instructors ask students to voluntarily provide their email address as part of the sign-up questions for their Facebook groups, this is treading in a gray area of Udemy policy however.

MailChimp charges you based on the size of your mailing list, so be judicious in who you add to it. People who give you their email address because they are engaged in your course are great, but people who just gave you an email address so they could get something free in return will be less valuable.

If you have a social media management tool such as HootSuite, you can also schedule your social media announcements in advance as well. Again, you will need to wait until you have a real coupon link to your course before you finalize the copy for these, so you might want to just draft out what you'll say someplace with a placeholder for the link when you have it. The effectiveness of marketing on Facebook and Twitter has been declining for me, though it doesn't cost anything to just make a post, so there's no good reason not to.

Social media management is a field upon itself, and cultivating a following for your courses requires a lot of constant work that goes beyond just trying to sell your stuff to people. You need to help people solve their problems, share useful information, and only occasionally ask for something in return. It's honestly not clear to me that all that effort is worthwhile; the number of sales I see that originate from social media are quite small. Just be judicious in the amount of time you invest in these channels.

If you have a blog or other web properties of your own, you also have an opportunity to blog about your new course. The real value of this is from an SEO perspective; the more links you can direct at your course landing page on Udemy, the more likely it is to come up in Google search results.

Since your focus is SEO, be sure to follow SEO best practices when writing these posts. If you're using WordPress, check out a plugin called Yoast SEO. It provides concrete advice about how well you're attacking the keywords you're trying to rank for, and whether you have enough text in your post for it to be effective.

Ideally new students will find your post before following it to Udemy – that way, you can claim 97% of the sale price by directing students to your course using your own coupon code, and you'll also boost your conversion rate on Udemy since the traffic you're sending is pre-qualified as highly interested in what you're offering.

If Udemy sees that your course converts well, its algorithms will know that it's a good investment for their own ad dollars, which will further boost your sales.

If you have more than one blog, don't just copy and paste the same post on multiple websites. Word it differently; write each one from scratch. Google can detect duplicate content, and it doesn't like to see it.

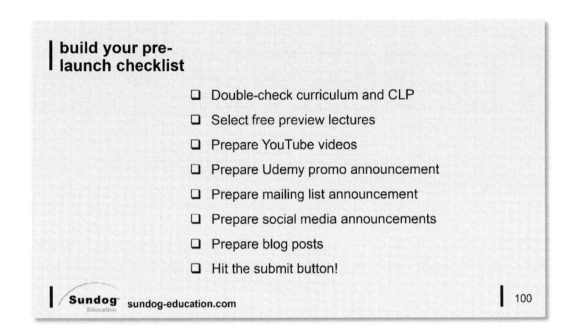

As an exercise, build your own pre-launch checklist and keep it handy. Your list may be different from mine. Perhaps there are specific social media platforms that you care about; perhaps you don't have a mailing list or a blog yet; perhaps you don't yet have existing students to send a promotional announcement to. But there will be some things you can do ahead of time so you'll be ready to start aggressively marketing your new course as soon as it's approved and on the platform.

The last step is to hit that "submit for review" button in your course editing dashboard, and wait for Udemy to publish it on the marketplace! Pushing that button is definitely cause for celebration!

Go ahead and draft your own pre-launch checklist, based on what we've covered. You'll find it gives you a lot of peace of mind, and the confidence you need to push that submit button once your content is ready to go.

build your post-launch checklist

- ☐ Create coupon codes
- ☐ Finalize and publish YouTube videos
- ☐ Finalize and send Udemy promo announcement
- ☐ Finalize and send mailing list announcement
- ☐ Finalize and publish social media announcements
- ☐ Finalize and publish blog posts
- ☐ *Profit* ☺

Sundog Education — sundog-education.com

While you're at, also create your personalized post-launch checklist. It's an exciting time when your new course hits the marketplace, and it's easy to forget the steps you need to complete in order to launch its initial marketing.

The first thing you need to do is create new coupon codes that you'll use with your initial promotions. You can create coupon codes in your course's "Price and Coupons" tab. It's best to create unique coupon codes for every marketing channel you're planning to use; one for YouTube, one for your mailing list, one for your promo announcement, etc. That way you can track how many sales are coming from each channel, and use that data to decide which channels to concentrate more on, and which ones aren't worth your time.

Udemy students have come to expect a price of $9.99, so you may as well embrace that and use that as the price on your launch coupons.

For each coupon, enter that price, set a really large number of each coupon like a million, and leave the deadline empty.

You don't want the coupon codes you're posting all over the Internet to expire or run out in the future. After you create each new coupon, Udemy offers to generate a link for you that you can use in your promotions.

When students follow that link, your $9.99 offer price will be automatically applied – and you'll automatically get 97% of that sale, provided an affiliate didn't tag your student first. Copy all of those links someplace so you'll have them handy while finalizing all of your launch promotions.

Now, it's just a matter of pasting in those links into the various announcements and video descriptions that you drafted ahead of launch, and publishing them. Paste your coupon link for YouTube into the description of the preview videos you plan to publish there, and publish them.

Insert your coupon link into your drafted Udemy promotional announcement, paste it into the Udemy promo announcement tool, send yourself a preview to make sure everything pasted in OK and all of your links work properly, and then send it out to your students.

Do the same with your mailing list, your social platforms, and your blog posts.

Be extra-careful with your Udemy promotional announcement. Their UI is notorious for doing bad things with content you've pasted into it, and if you send out a mistake, you can't correct it without burning through another one of the two announcements you're allowed per month.

Preview it, proofread it, and test it in every way you can before pushing the button to send it out to everyone. This will be the most effective marketing tool in your arsenal, and it's important to not mess it up.

Then, there's nothing left to do for now, just sit back and wait for those first few students to enroll! However, your rest will be short-lived – there's still a lot of work you need to do to maintain your course and ensure it continues to sell for years to come.

We'll start covering that in our next section.

Promoting your new course after it is completed and launched has worked well enough for me, but it's worth mentioning that there are alternative approaches as well.

One is crowdfunding; using sites such as Kickstarter or IndieGoGo to actually convince people to pay for your course before you've even made it. A lot of marketers like this approach because it allows you to validate the demand for your course before you invest any time into it. If your Kickstarter doesn't make its initial funding goal, you can choose to just not make the course and try a different idea.

Some of the larger instructors on Udemy have done this repeatedly with some success. It also has the advantage of giving their new course a huge launch on Udemy once it's ready, when all of those initial backers redeem their free coupons to take the course when it's released.

I asked Udemy once if that sort of thing is within their policies, and they are in fact OK with selling on Kickstarter in this manner. Udemy's stance is that it's bringing new students onto the platform, and they're just fine with that – even if they aren't making any money on the initial enrollments that came from Kickstarter backers.

Crafting a successful crowdfunding campaign is a science unto itself, however. If your Kickstarter doesn't take off, it doesn't necessarily mean there's no demand for your course on Udemy. It might just mean that you're not good at creating compelling Kickstarter campaigns. I also don't like this approach because if you do meet your funding goals, you now have a lot of promises to fulfill to a lot of people, and they're going to become very angry if you don't deliver on them. Part of why I like being a Udemy instructor is the personal freedom it gives you – but when you're on the hook to produce a new course by a certain date for people who already paid money for it, that's exactly the sort of stress I'm trying to avoid in life.

It's also possible to pre-sell a course and give it a boost at launch entirely on the Udemy platform, however, and in a way that isn't stressful for you as an instructor. The idea is to wait until you're almost done with a course, and then publish the bulk of it in "private" status on Udemy. When you publish a course on Udemy in private status, the only people who can enroll are the people you've given a password to.

If you have an existing following off Udemy, through a mailing list or social media, you can offer them an "early access" password that allows them to start consuming your course before it's even done.

Over the next few weeks, you keep uploading new content until you're ready to publish the course in public status. And if you're lucky, those early access students have given you some enrollments and positive reviews before your course even launches. They might also have discovered some issues in your course that you were able to fix prior to its public launch.

This sounds like a great idea, and I did try it once myself. The thing is, if you have a large enough following to pull that off, you're probably not going to have much trouble getting a new course off the ground anyhow. The course I offered private, early access to, ultimately did not perform any better than my other courses where I didn't do that. In the end, I don't think it's worth the trouble – though it is an interesting thing to try out if you have enough followers.

Another launch strategy is to make a bunch of free coupons for your new course, and give them out all over the place in hopes that it will drive some enrollments and reviews in your new course.

This is almost always a bad idea. Yes, you can get lots of enrollments very quickly this way – but the vast majority of those new students have no real interest in what you're teaching; they just hoard free stuff. The few who do look at your course probably don't have the pre-requisite skills needed for it, and are likely to be frustrated by it and may leave poor reviews as a result. There is also a weird effect where people tend to value things based on how much they paid for it. The course they received for free has no real value to them, and so they don't hesitate to quickly discard it and leave a bad review.

The more someone pays for something, the better the reviews they leave for it. It's because people don't want to admit that they wasted their money on something. But if they got it for free, it doesn't reflect poorly on their own choices if they don't like it.

Udemy isn't stupid, either. They know which enrollments and reviews came from free students, and they weight them appropriately. Those free students won't do as much good as you think.

If you do cave into the temptation to issue free coupons to give your new course some initial life, at least be judicious in where you distribute them. If you just put them on general coupon sites, it will just result in your course getting stolen by people re-selling it, or in it ending up on a pirate site. At least find online communities that are relevant to your topic, and offer them there to people who might have a genuine interest in what you're teaching. Even if you can find such a community, it's rare that they allow self-promotion – so check with the administrators of those communities first.

Matching your course with the right students is the key to getting good reviews, and the early reviews on your course can result in its success or failure. I avoid giving out free coupons like the plague now. If you must use them, use them carefully.

CHAPTER 9 – Marketing Your Course

One of the most common questions on Udemy's instructor communities is "how do I market my new course?" For new instructors, this is both critical and difficult. Let me talk you through some proven strategies I've tried myself, and also talk about what doesn't work so you don't waste your time or money. In the end, you'll develop your own launch plan for your course to make sure you don't leave any opportunities on the table.

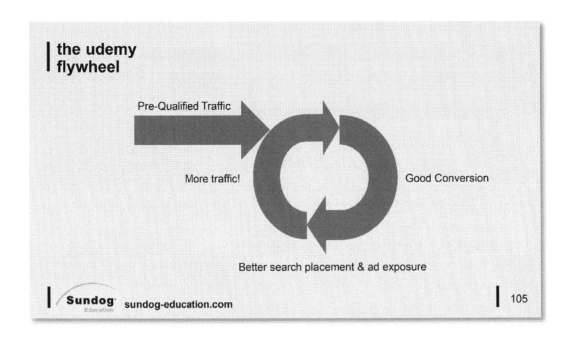

To be successful with Udemy, it helps to view your presence on the platform as a business that you run. And one of the more powerful concepts in business is called the "Flywheel Effect." The idea was introduced in a book called "Good to Great," and it also played a big role in Amazon.com's growth.

The idea is to look for self-sustaining cycles in businesses, and way to fuel those cycles over time to make them "spin" faster and faster. It's possible to view the sales of your course on Udemy through this lens. Let's walk our way through this diagram, as it's worth understanding.

Let's start on the left. This arrow going into the flywheel represents any pre-qualified traffic you can send into your course landing page on Udemy. This might be coupon links from your YouTube video descriptions, from your blog, from your Udemy promotional announcements, or your social media posts about your course.

This traffic is "pre-qualified" because people would only follow those links if they had a genuine interest in your course, so the people coming to your course landing page are pretty likely to actually purchase it. This sort of traffic can generate conversion rates of around 20%, which is way, way higher than conversion rates you get from random people just browsing the Udemy platform.

So, by infusing your course landing page with pre-qualified traffic from your own marketing, you can boost the overall conversion rate of your course landing page. That's what we mean by "good conversion" as we enter the flywheel.

Conversion rate is an important signal to Udemy's algorithms. It is only economical for them to purchase online ads for courses that have high conversion rates, for one thing. Udemy pays for clicks to course landing pages, and they want to send those clicks to the pages most likely to result in a purchase that will recoup the cost of that ad. Courses that convert well will be advertised more heavily by Udemy. It's also a signal to Udemy's search algorithms to students like what they see when they reach your landing page, and good conversions can also boost your search placement on Udemy.

What happens with better search placement and more ads for your course? More traffic to your course landing page! And as that increased traffic leads to even more conversions and hopefully a higher conversion rate on your course, Udemy just keeps promoting it more and more for you. In practice, there is an upper bound to how fast this flywheel can spin for an individual instructor – your job is to get it spinning as fast as you can.

Creating a compelling course landing page keeps this flywheel working efficiently, but to give it an extra push, you need to constantly feed it with new, pre-qualified traffic of your own.

Why is this such an important insight? Well, for one thing it informs the strategy of sending all of your external marketing to your course landing page on Udemy – not to your own website, or to some other platform. The traffic you send to Udemy is worth more than just the initial sale it might drive; it helps to keep sending signals to Udemy's algorithms to keep promoting your course for you, on your behalf. And the reach of Udemy's marketing tools far outweigh your own. The key to success on Udemy is keeping its algorithms happy, by showing Udemy that people who visit your course landing page are likely to buy it.

Conversion rate isn't the only signal, of course. Reviews matter too, as well as your SEO strategy. Maintaining good conversion rates by sending pre-qualified traffic to your course is something that requires sustained effort and discipline; it's not like SEO where you can just improve your landing page and call it good. Spinning a flywheel requires continued effort, pushing in a consistent direction.

Just about every successful instructor you talk to will say that you need to put in persistent hard work over a long period of time to get there, and this is why.

Let's talk about how to keep that pre-qualified traffic pushing your flywheel forward.

ongoing promotional announcements

- Send twice per month
- Rotate amongst promos for each course
- Send to anyone not currently enrolled in it
- Send a promo of a related course to those who are enrolled in it

The most effective tool you have for pushing that flywheel forward are the promotional emails Udemy will send on your behalf. But this only works if you have more than one course – so if you don't, the first thing you should be focused on is launching a second course!

If you do have multiple courses – you're able to send a promotional email twice a month to the students enrolled in each of your courses, to promote your other courses to them. In reality many students opt out of these emails, but it's still your best audience. These are people who already gave you money to learn from you, and are likely to do so again. If you can get these people to look at the course landing page for your other courses, they're quite likely to purchase them – which fuels your conversion rate, and keeps the flywheel spinning.

Logistically, here's what I do. I have a recurring calendar reminder in the middle of every month, and near the end of every month, to remind me to send out Udemy promotional announcements. This way I take full advantage of the two promotional emails per course, per month, that Udemy allows.

Every time that calendar reminder pops up, I send out the next group of promotional announcements that I have pre-written in this big Google Docs document, so I can just copy and paste them into Udemy's announcement editor – after proofreading that the paste went in successfully.

Each "group" rotates through every course I offer, so every couple of weeks I'm primarily just promoting the next course in my list of courses to all of my existing students who are not currently enrolled in it. That's also wasting an opportunity to promote to the students who are enrolled in course I'm promoting in this cycle. So, I'll send out a second promotional announcement just to students who are currently enrolled in the primary course I'm promoting, advertising a course related to the one they are taking. Let me phrase that a little differently, as it confuses a lot of people. Twice a month, I'll send out two promotional emails.

One promoting the next course in a rotating list of all of my courses to all students not currently enrolled in it, and another promoting a related course to the students who are currently enrolled in it.

Or even more simply: whenever it's time send out promotional announcements, I move to the next course in my list, send a promo announcement to students who are not enrolled in it, and another promo announcement for a related course to those who are enrolled in it.

The reason I rotate through all of my courses in a never-ending cycle is so I can give a little boost to the flywheel of all of them on a periodic basis. Over time, there may be some courses you don't want to promote any longer because they've gotten out of date or something, and you would just remove them from this rotation.

You could be even more strategic, and send promo announcements more frequently to the courses with the lowest conversion rates. The "performance" tab in your instructor dashboard allows you to see the actual conversion rates for all of your courses, and it can inform you which of your courses' flywheels need a boost the most. I prefer to keep it simple however, and just maintain a fixed rotation amongst them all.

We talked about crafting effective promotional announcements earlier, but the main tips are to communicate the benefit and opportunity you're offering in the title and early in the text of the announcement, and have links from your coupon code to the course in the announcement early and often. Don't focus on the specific topics you're teaching; focus on the value you're offering to the student.

Remember, you'll send your promotional announcements from your Udemy instructor dashboard, via the "Create New" button. Be very careful to select a promotional announcement, and not an educational announcement – as sending promotional messages through educational announcements can land you in a lot of trouble. A reminder, be careful when you're pasting pre-written text into Udemy's announcement editor. It often messes up formatting and links, and you really need to double-check everything and proofread a test email before you send it out.

Promotional announcements work great if you have more than one course, but what if you don't?

Well, these days you're probably better off creating that second course so you can start taking advantage of the power of cross-promotion. There is one other trick however, and it's part of how I got started with my first course.

The idea is to create a shorter, free course that's directly related to your paid course – and promote your paid course in the final "bonus lecture" of the free course. Udemy does not allow you to send promotional emails to students in free courses, so the bonus lecture is the only place where you can promote your larger, paid course to those students.

For example, you might create a free course that covers the pre-requisite skills needed for your larger, paid course. Students who finish the free course will see your paid course as a natural next step for them, giving a boost to that paid course's flywheel in the process.

Free courses do have a tendency to be rated lower than paid courses, but this isn't always the case. If your free course is well produced and delivers real, tangible value to the student, it can still end up reviewed favorably. Another downside is that students might start to expect everything from you for free, and it devalues your content to some extent. You'll also have to provide Q&A support for this free course, in exchange for nothing. The good thing about a free course is that if it ends up doing more harm than good, you can just un-publish it and be done with it. It's not like free coupons, where if they end up driving poor reviews on the course you're trying to sell, there's nothing you can do to reverse that.

Most instructors and Udemy frown upon building free courses, but it's a strategy you might want to consider in order to give your first course a boost. Just be sure to give it sufficient time; the vast majority of people who enroll in free courses are just hoarding free stuff and will never actually take your course – and of the few who do, even fewer will make it all the way to the end where they will see your promotion for your paid course. This is a strategy that will take months to see an effect from, so don't give up on it too soon. A free course is also a great lead generation tool to lure people into a sales funnel, which we'll talk about next.

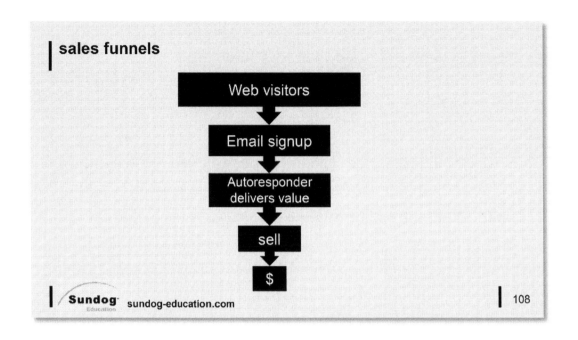

You might hear a lot about "funnels" when it comes to online marketing. Unfortunately, some of it is just hype; there is a popular software package called "ClickFunnels" that uses something akin to a multi-level-marketing scheme to entice people to sell it in exchange for a commission. A lot of people you hear talking about how great sales funnels are, are just trying to make a profit from you. It is a legitimate idea however, and in many situations, it can be an effective sales tool.

The general idea is to view a customer's journey toward purchasing your course as a funnel. You have a lot of people visiting your website, and some percentage of those people sign up for your mailing list. To entice them to do so, you might use a "lead magnet" such as a free course or a free e-book that they receive in exchange for signing up.

Then you deliver a series of automatic responses to that new subscriber, giving them the free stuff you promised, and just generally being helpful to them for awhile by providing them more tips and tricks. After a few weeks or so, you then hit them up with an "ask" to buy your course. By this point, the idea goes, they will be so indebted to you for all the free stuff and advice you've given them, that they'll feel obligated to purchase your course at this point.

If you can get a system like this working, you can just focus on getting more people into the top your "funnel", and increasing the conversion rates at each stage of the funnel. That is, try to maximize the number of web visitors who sign up for your list, and maximize the number of list subscribers who ultimately respond to your call to action for a purchase down the road. When it works, it's basically a money machine.

I've used MailChimp to set up a system like this on my own website, however it drives very few sales. I don't think the sales it drives even pays for MailChimp's monthly fees. The reason is that sales funnels don't really make a lot of sense for $10 purchases of a course.

If you have some sort of larger, more expensive product or service that you're trying to sell in addition to your Udemy courses, perhaps a sales funnel makes more sense for you.

Here's the problem – the main way to drive traffic into the top of your funnel is via online ads. But the economics of online ads don't make sense for such inexpensive items as a Udemy course.

If you pay 50 cents per click to your website, you will need impossibly good conversion rates for people signing up to your email list and subsequently purchasing from it in order to recoup that ad expense.

So you can only rely on free, organic traffic going into your funnel, which is generally very small. Only a tiny percentage of that traffic ends up coming out of the bottom of your funnel, with an actual purchase of your course.

The other thing is that a $10 course is really more of an impulse purchase. You don't necessarily need to "build a relationship" with a customer before they will hand over $10 for a comprehensive 10-hour course on some skill they need to acquire. If you're trying to get them to sign up for a $20,000 coaching package or something, then that's different. A funnel might just be adding too much friction for what should be a snap decision from someone looking at your courses.

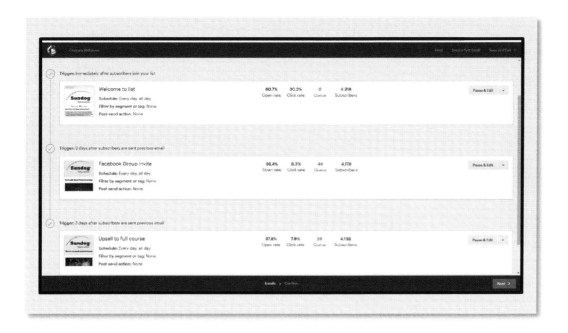

That said, it's not expensive to try setting up a funnel if you have your own website, and something like a MailChimp account. Again, I use MailChimp, and this is what the setup looks like for the automated workflow I set up for my own funnel.

When someone signs up for my mailing list on my website, the first thing they receive is an email giving them the free course I'm offering as a "lead magnet" to entice people to sign up. 3 days after that, they receive an invitation to join a Facebook group related to this course, which gives them even more free resources. And 3 days after that, I send them the actual ask to check out my paid courses on Udemy.

You can see how quickly the numbers dwindle as you work your way down the funnel.

Only 60% of people even open the email that's sent when they sign up, and of those, only 30% actually click to receive their free course. By the time they reach the end of my funnel, only 8% of the 37% still opening my emails actually look at my courses on Udemy – and an even smaller percentage end up actually purchasing them once they are there.

It's still pretty cool that this is a fully automated system for driving sales online, and if I were selling a higher-priced item, it would become economical to invest in paid ads to drive more people into it. But for $10 courses, it just isn't effective to buy ads to scale this funnel up.

It does drive a few sales here and there just from free, organic traffic however, and that's about all you should expect if you set up something similar. It's not going to push your flywheel forward in any meaningful way, but every little bit helps.

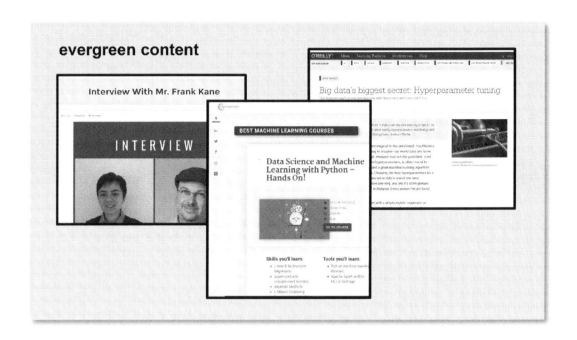

Another way to keep pushing your flywheel forward is to write as much content as you can all over the web, with some sort of link that leads to your course on Udemy. If someone wants to publish an interview with me, the answer is yes! If someone wants to add my course to their "top-10" list of courses, sure! If O'Reilly wants me to guest-blog for them, absolutely!

These are additional places on the Internet where someone can be introduced to me, and ultimately find my courses. The people who do follow those links are predisposed to be interested in my course, and are more likely to purchase it – driving my flywheel of conversion on Udemy.

I call this "evergreen content," because once you've put in the effort to write whatever is needed for this content, it just sits there forever doing its job of funneling new students your way while you sleep. It's also a strong signal to Google to rank your course higher when people are searching for it.

When you're starting, you'll have to actively seek out these sorts of opportunities, as they won't just come to you until you're established. It's not that hard, really. Find a news or community site relevant to what you are teaching, and offer to write a guest-blog article for it.

You can publish your own articles on platforms such as Medium or LinkedIn. Maybe you have a personal blog of your own, where you can put some content related to what you teach. Those are all opportunities to get your name out there that are completely under your control. As long as you have a link to your course somewhere in there, it'll do its job.

Don't focus this content on selling your course, though. Nobody will find that interesting. A better approach is to write an article that actually provides some sort of useful information to the reader that's relevant to what you teach, and just have a quick mention of your course in there somewhere.

Make the focus of your content delivering some real value to the reader, not selling your course. People are sick of being sold to all of the time, and they'll appreciate it if your approach is subtle and friendly in nature.

Many new instructors look to paid advertising on Facebook or Google as a way to get their new course off the ground.

My advice is: this is just throwing money away.

I've tried this myself several times, and many other instructors have reported the same results I found: there is no way to make money buying online ads for a $10 course on Udemy. You will end up spending more than $10 for every purchase that results from your ads.

Let's say you are spending $1 per click on an ad for your course – you'd have to convert one out of every 10 clicks into a sale just to break even, which is a conversion rate of 10%. In practice, that is impossibly high. You're lucky to get a 1% conversion rate from paid ads, even with all of the targeting available today.

There's just too much fraud and too many accidental clicks for the math to work out in your favor. Sure, your ad might get a lot of "likes" – but those "likes" are worthless.

It's cost-effective for Udemy to run ads on your behalf, because the lifetime value of a new student is much more to them than it is to you as an individual instructor. Even Udemy is struggling to make ads work effectively. It's not just them; the effectiveness of online advertising has been becoming worse over the past several years, and there's no sign of that trend reversing. If you think about it too much, it makes you want to go build a bunker in the desert so you can survive the impending economic collapse. It's best not to think about it! Just don't get into the world of online advertising. Like sales funnels, it only makes sense if you're selling more expensive goods and services. At a $10 price point, just let Udemy do the advertising for you. That's why you're giving them a cut of your revenue, after all.

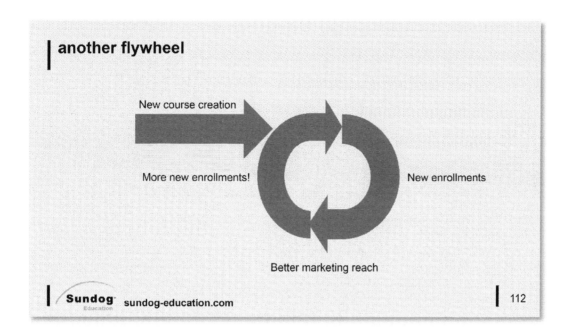

While we're talking about the power of flywheel effects, there is another flywheel process you can use to your advantage on Udemy. This is simply the power of making new courses. If you want to make more money on Udemy, the answer is almost always to just make more courses.

Every new course you create will attract some new students. And those are more students that you can target in your promotional announcements to sell your other courses to, resulting in even more enrollments. The more courses you make, the bigger your audience, and the more enrollments you can drive. It's kind of like compound interest; every new course you make will have a larger and larger audience that you can market it to directly.

It's really that simple. Success on Udemy becomes easier and easier as you release more and more courses on the platform.

Over time, the sales you generate just from this flywheel effect, Udemy promotional announcements, and the marketing Udemy does on your behalf will be all you really need.

The other marketing techniques we discussed will generate smaller and smaller results in comparison to what the Udemy platform gives you on its own. Ultimately, you can stop worrying about marketing, and focus instead on just making more courses. It's another example of where persistence over a long period of time pays off.

> **build your ongoing marketing plan**
>
> - Where can I write articles that link back to my course?
> - Does a funnel make sense for me?
> - Should I make a free course to attract new students?
> - What is my promo announcement strategy?

Take what we've covered in this section, and apply it to your own situation. Everyone can write content on the Internet and link back to your courses; there's no excuse for not doing that. Make a list of the platforms and related websites where you can blog or guest-blog, and think up some topics you can write about that are directly related to what you teach.

Sales funnels are only effective if you have an existing website that has a fair amount of traffic coming into it already. If you don't have that, then don't bother. But if you do, you might want to plan on setting up a funnel using MailChimp on your site – so plan out the details of that.

Is this your first course? If so, is there a short, free course you can release that will directly lead into your paid course as a natural extension? Perhaps producing that course is something you want to try out.

If it's not your first course, make your own schedule for releasing promotional announcements twice per month, to give all of your courses a periodic boost in conversion, and keep their flywheels spinning.

Give yourself calendar reminders, and have your content all written up and ready to go so it's just a matter of copying and pasting when that reminder comes up.

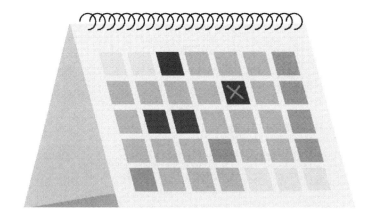

CHAPTER 10 – Maintaining Your Course

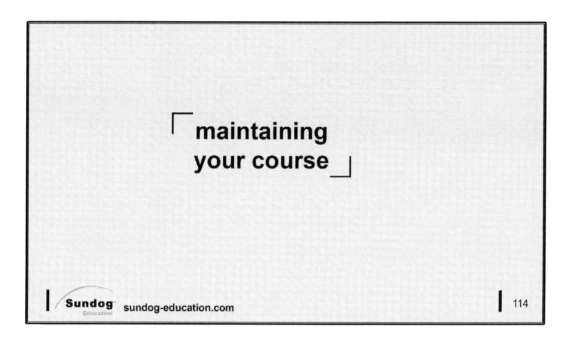

O nce you've launched your course, you may feel like you've deserved a break - but the work has only just begun! In order to turn your course into a sustainable source of residual income, you need to keep working at maintaining and promoting it. Udemy isn't really "passive income" - it does require ongoing effort. Let's talk about what you should be doing in the long term, and how to manage that work.

managing q&a

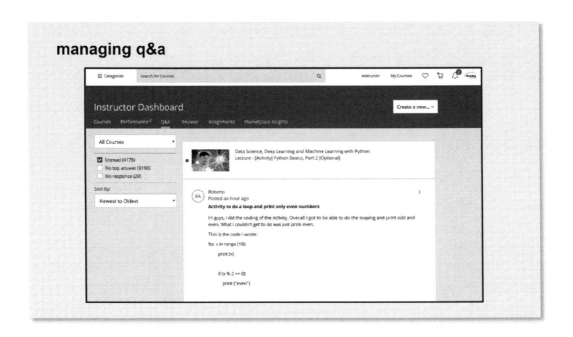

Udemy's Q&A feature is the main reason Udemy income is not passive. Part of why students pay for Udemy courses is the direct line they have to the instructor to ask questions. If you don't answer those questions in a timely manner, you will get punished with low reviews on your course.

You can't just launch a course and forget about it. You need to check for new questions on your course at least once a day, and also look for follow-up questions that the student may have left as a reply to your answer. It can be a bit of a chore, however it's an opportunity to build a personal connection with these students, and try to earn a good review from them.

Here's a tip: don't just look at the unanswered questions in your instructor dashboard. Check the notification icon – that's the little bell icon in the upper right corner of the dashboard – to ensure you also see any responses to the answers you already left.

At Sundog Education, we're always careful to answer every new question within 24 hours – but sometimes we miss follow-up questions, and end up with poor reviews as a result. You need to be diligent in looking for new problems your students are having, whether they are new questions or replies to the answers you gave.

Q&A is also a great way to find out if something is wrong with your course. Especially with technical topics, the technology you're teaching may change quickly, and the way you originally recorded working with it may not work for long. If a student says "I did what you said in the lecture and it didn't work," don't automatically assume that the student just can't follow instructions.

Try it again yourself and see if you need to update your lecture to keep up with changes in the world. If you find yourself getting the same questions repeatedly, then you should address that question in the content of the course itself. Edit your lecture videos to incorporate the answers to the questions that keep coming up, so you can spend less time on Q&A and your students can have a better experience.

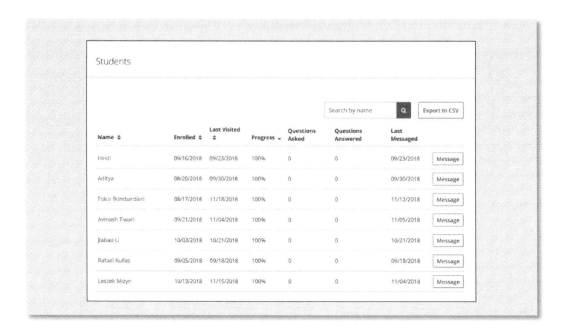

Once you have enough students, Q&A can start to become a real burden. If you have so many students that you can't find enough time in the day to answer their questions, this is what we call a good problem to have. Fortunately, there is a solution – hire a teaching assistant, or maybe even several teaching assistants, to answer questions so you don't have to. Teaching assistants are called "TA" for short.

If you click on the number of students for any given course in your instructor dashboard, you'll be taken to this Students screen. In it, you can view all of the students enrolled in your course, and click on the "Progress" column to find all of the students who have completed the course.

If you see a student who completed your course, and has also been answering questions themselves in Q&A on their own initiative, they are a good candidate for being a TA for that course.

You can also export this list to a CSV file, so you can sort it in Excel or something to more easily identify the students who both completed your course and are active in Q&A anyhow.

You can hit the "message" button next to anyone in this list to communicate with them directly, and see if they might be interested in working part-time as your TA. You might be surprised at how often they say yes! Of course, there has to be something in it for them, and you need to come up with some form of fair compensation for their time. Someone working for free probably won't be reliable, because they have no reason to be.

Here's how I worked things out with my own TA. After identifying my best, most-engaged student, I reached out to him and asked if he'd be interested. Much to my luck, he was. We decided to do a one-week trial where he would take over Q&A. This involves adding the student as a co-instructor on the course, with permissions only for Q&A, so he can see questions on your course in his dashboard.

After that one week, I looked at his work and decided he was doing a good job – and he was still interested in doing it. I then asked how much time ended up spending on Q&A during that week, and what a fair amount would be to compensate him for that time. So, we had number of what that week's Q&A handling would cost for him.

Since you probably don't want to actually hire a TA as an employee, what you can then do is look at your total revenue for that week, and divide the TA's expected payment by it to arrive at a percentage split of your overall revenue for that course that would fairly compensate your TA. Then, you can just assign your TA a revenue share as a co-instructor at whatever that split works out to be. It's great because as your student base grows and your Q&A workload increases, your TA will automatically get paid more as your revenue increases.

Occasionally, your TA will need to escalate a question to you, however for the most part, having a TA will allow you to spend that time you were spending on Q&A support on creating new courses instead.

Now, you really should answer Q&A yourself for as long as you can. Nobody can provide better answers for your courses than you, and getting 1:1 support from the instructor is a really positive student experience that leads to good reviews. If you find yourself spending hours every day dealing with Q&A, and dreading looking at your instructor dashboard because of all the work it has waiting for you – it's time to get a TA.

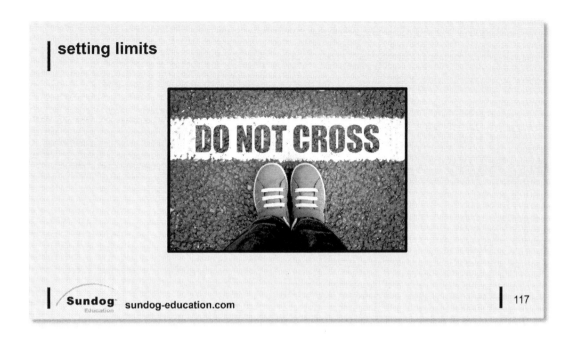

It's also important to set limits when dealing with student contacts, such as Q&A. There are some students who will view you as their personal tutor for life in exchange for the $5 or so you received from them.

Every day, I receive demands from students who want me to consult with them on their projects at work or at school, and that's just not part of the deal.

You have to become good at politely saying "no." Something like "I'm sorry, but with thousands of students I just don't have the time to help people out with their projects outside of the course itself. I invite you to post your question on (the course's Facebook group / StackOverflow / some other relevant resource) to see if you can find the help you need there. Hope you understand!"

There will be students who want to call you on the phone, have live chats, and share their screens with you. Don't go down that path, because students like that will just want more and more over time. If you want to offer paid consulting services, you can always offer that as an option for them – if not, you just have to say no. Yes, you are risking a negative review by doing this, but it's very rare for that to happen as a result, provided you are polite when you say no.

You may want to be helpful to people, just remember you can be the most helpful by scaling out your knowledge to as many people as you can. You literally do not have enough hours in the day to help out every student individually. You'll do much more good in the world spending your time creating more content that can teach thousands of people around the world all at the same time, than by spending your time working with individuals on a 1:1 basis.

Perhaps the most difficult part of maintaining your course is dealing with reviews. Everyone receives one-star reviews from time to time, and it always hurts. It can be extremely discouraging and demotivating when someone leaves scathing, and sometimes personal, attacks for you online for the world to see. This is probably the toughest rite of passage for new instructors, and honestly it never gets much easier.

I will tell you that if you're getting a lot of bad reviews, and your average is less than 4.0, you should probably swallow your pride and listen to what they are trying to say. There may be a real issue with your presentation style, audio quality, depth of information presented, or something – and if so, the text in those reviews are probably telling you what you need to fix. At least learn from what they're saying, and apply it to your next course. Reviews at their best provide constructive criticism that help you to be a better instructor. You may not want to hear it, but it's important to learn from it.

> **what do reviews really mean?**
>
> - How <u>difficult</u> is your course?
> - How <u>likable</u> are you?
> - <u>How much</u> did the student pay for your course?
> - How <u>new</u> is your course?
> - What is the <u>international breakdown</u> of your students?

If you're only getting bad reviews occasionally, and you're maintaining an average above 4.0 – there's a good chance that there's nothing to be concerned about.

You really can't make everyone happy, and the truth is that reviews are not a perfect measure of a course's actual quality. What they measure is often something else entirely.

I've got a lot of data to work with - my 10 courses have yielded tens of thousands of reviews. Yet, the range of average review scores on these courses is just from 4.45 to 4.53. I'm much more proud of some courses than others - and my very first ones really make me cringe. However, their reviews don't reflect this at all. The course I'm most proud of actually has the lowest score.

I'm not alone in questioning the usefulness of star reviews; Netflix recently decided to abandon star reviews altogether. They found actual user behavior to be a much better signal, as reviews are too easily gamed and subject to biases. In studying other courses on Udemy's platform, I've found that pretty much any well-constructed technical course will have a rating of around 4.5. The slight variations around 4.5 have very little to do with the course itself, but are more a measure of things you might not expect:

How difficult is your course?

The course I'm most proud of is also the most challenging course. On an open platform such as Udemy, there's no way to enforce pre-requisites for a given course. Although my course on data science and machine learning clearly states that you need to have some programming and mathematical background in order to be successful, it doesn't stop people from enrolling who don't have the necessary experience.

When students eager to learn highly valuable skills enroll in this course, yet find themselves struggling, their instinct is not to blame themselves- they'll blame you. Your course moved too quickly; setting things up was too difficult; more explanation of the basics was needed. And your punishment will be a one-star review, which as an outlier can really bring down your average quickly.

The opposite effect can also be a factor - if a self-proclaimed expert in the field you are teaching just wants to make himself look smart at your expense, a one-star review may be more about serving his ego than anything else.

How likable are you as an instructor?

How do I explain that all of my courses have roughly the same review score? I think students are rating the instructor, and his presentation skills, more so than the content of the course itself. I am the one common factor across these courses.

Think about every time you've received an evaluation form at the end of a conventional class in a classroom. You figure the instructor probably had very little to do with developing the course curriculum, materials, and setting up the A/V equipment. You're evaluating how much you liked the instructor, and how engaging he or she was.

Online instructors spend the vast majority of their time developing all those behind-the-scenes aspects of their courses, and spend relatively little time actually presenting the material. That presentation is what's primarily being evaluated. If you want to boost your review scores, improve your presentation skills. Poorly reviewed courses on Udemy invariably have very dry presentation.

This also means instructors who have an accent that is foreign to their audience on Udemy are at an inherent disadvantage, and reviews are also subject to cultural biases that students may not even be fully aware of.

How much did your students pay for your course?

I've noticed a direct relationship between the amount of money a student pays for the course, and the review score they leave. Lower price points attract impulse buyers who don't think enough about whether this course is really appropriate for their skill level. It also creates less of a sense of personal investment in the course, which can yield lower effort in taking it. When a student feels like they have very little to lose by failing at your course, it often becomes a self-fulfilling prophecy. And of course, they'll blame you and not themselves for this.

How new is your course?

The first thing an instructor does when releasing a new course is promote it to his existing students from other courses. This yields an initial flood of reviews from his biggest fans, and most loyal customers.

Udemy however only looks at reviews over a 3-month sliding window. So once that initial burst of love passes the 3-month mark, your reviews will be coming more from students who have discovered you for the first time, and are not pre-disposed to enjoy your content. Often the difference between a 4.6 and a 4.5 review score is simply that the 4.6-rated course came out within the last 3 months.

What is the international breakdown of your students?

There is a huge variation in average reviews given by students in different countries. My data science course has been translated to German, Japanese, and Korean. The same course that gets a 4.5 in English only gets a 4.1 in German and 3.8 in Japanese. I've also observed that almost every negative review on my English courses come from students in India.

Different countries have different cultures, and different standards on what a 5-star review really represents. There are also differences in educational systems that may lead to students from some countries struggling more with your course than others. And, language barrier issues can also prevent students from being successful. Again, it doesn't matter why a student wasn't successful - they will blame you for it, and reflect that in their review.

Review scores are not the pure measures of quality they appear to be. They measure many other things that are largely outside of your control as an instructor.

However, there are some things you can do. Be really explicit in your early lectures about the pre-requisites for your course, and direct students to places where they can learn them. Speak clearly and offer quality subtitles for your international students. Keep promoting your portfolio of courses to your existing students to get more ratings from your fans. Hone your presentation skills and only record when your energy is at its highest. The actual content of your course is less important that you think. Understanding what really drives review scores can help you create a better experience for all of your students.

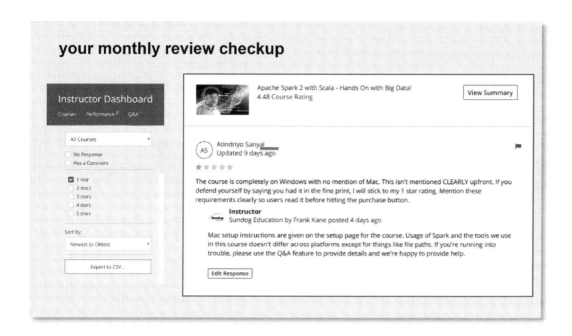

Even though reviews are not a perfect measure of a course's true quality, we have to live with the reality that they still have an impact on sales, and we need to manage them as best we can.

Reading negative reviews is a painful experience. I find it's better to just deal with all of them all at once, just once per month. It's just easier on your mental health to only read about how much you suck as infrequently as possible. Some instructors even hire an assistant to deal with responding to reviews so they don't have to. Again, if your average is under 4.0 then there are likely some very real issues with your course, and those reviews might contain stuff you need to know in order to make your course and future courses better. A poorly reviewed course won't sell well, and if it is in fact your fault, you're going to have to face up to that. If you know your course is on the whole well received, you can justify minimizing your exposure to negative feedback.

Every month, I go to my instructor dashboard, select the Reviews tab, and filter for one- and two-star reviews. This will bring up a rather painful view of all of your worst reviews, sorted by recency.

Most of them won't say anything; I see a lot of one-star reviews where the student gave positive feedback on all of the questions asked, and no review text was left. Sometimes, people just hit the wrong button, or don't understand how reviews work. But you can't prove that's what happened, so there's nothing you can do about things like that.

Focus on the reviews where the student actually wrote something. What you're hoping to find are negative reviews that Udemy's policy team will remove if you flag them. For example, if a student leaves a one-star review due to a video streaming issue, or an issue with the Udemy platform itself, that's not your fault. If you hit the flag icon next to that review and explain that, Udemy will likely remove that review, and it will no longer count toward your average. Sometimes a negative review will be accompanied by text complaining about being asked to review the course at such an early point.

Once I had a one-star review that just contained the word "No." It turns out that when a student is prompted to leave a review on Udemy, they get a pop-up that says "would you like to leave a review now?" This student just hit one star and typed "no" because they did not want to leave a review. I flagged it, and Udemy removed it.

A review that is abusive or a personal attack on you is a violation of Udemy's policies as well. If a student really crosses the line into abusive behavior, you can flag that as well. Ultimately it will be a judgment call, though there's a chance Udemy will remove those too.

That will leave you with reviews such as the one shown here. In this example, a student left a one-star review because I recorded the course on the Windows platform, and the student uses a Mac. The course does include instructions on how to use it on a Mac, but the student was angry that I used Windows instead. In this case, no policy was violated, and the student is complaining about an aspect of the course itself.

Udemy's stance is that this student is entitled to their opinion, no matter how unreasonable it may seem, and this isn't the sort of review you should even bother having removed. Instead, the correct response is to take a deep breath, and write a polite response explaining why this student's concern is not a valid reason for new prospective students to avoid the course. I explained that the course can in fact be used on a Mac, and instructions for doing so are part of the course materials. I'm not going to bother trying to argue with the student who left this review; my only objective is to address the concern the student raised so that it won't prevent new students reading this review from purchasing the course. You really need to be careful to not sound defensive in your responses to negative reviews. Just state the facts, try to be helpful, and thank the student for their feedback.

In cases where a poor review is a result of an actual problem with your course, the best reaction is to fix that problem, and respond to the review saying you've fixed it. That way, no prospective student will be put off by the review.

Some instructors respond to each and every review, good and bad. I don't really see the value in doing this – it's the bad reviews that do the damage, and those need to be the ones you're focused on mitigating.

After you read all of these bad reviews, you're not going to feel very good about yourself. So, it's a good idea to follow-up this exercise by looking at all the five-star reviews instead! Hopefully, you'll have a much larger 5-star review amount than 1-stars anyways, and it's good to remind yourself of that!

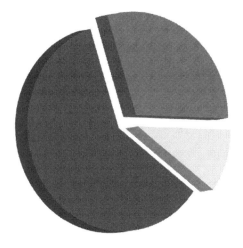

how reviews work

- Your review average is not an average
- Reviews lose weight over a 3 month period
- Written reviews count more
- The progress of the student in your course counts
- Reviews must pass a filter

It's worth understanding how Udemy's review system works, as it's not really intuitive. Udemy realized on their own that there wasn't a good correlation between a course's review scores and more objective measures of the quality of a course, such as student engagement.

In other words, they know that reviews don't really measure the quality of a course. As such, they have manipulated how they calculate a course's review score in such a manner to make your average review score correlate better with student engagement metrics.

Your average review score is not actually an average of all of your reviews; it's more complicated than that, and understanding how it works can inform how you think about any individual review you might receive.

First of all, reviews only count toward your average for 3 months. Many instructors get confused when their review score suddenly changes for no apparent reason, or in a direction they didn't expect. Usually, it's because a review passed that 3-month mark and stopped being counted toward your average. If a student left a scathing one-star review, after three months that review will no longer count, and you should see your average increase again at that point.

Conversely, if a five-star review falls over that 3-month cliff, it will bring your review score down a little bit. On the whole this is a good thing, because it means that if you do have negative feedback and you address that feedback with revisions to your course, it will at least have another chance at a good review score after 3 months have passed.

No matter what's going on with the reviews on your course, in 3 months you'll be working from a clean slate again.

We also know that written reviews count more than reviews that are just a star rating with no text. So, don't get nervous about those one-star reviews that have no text with them. Yes, they may well have been left by accident – but they don't actually count all that much toward your score.

Also, the progress of the student in your course counts. A student who reviews your course after completing it will count much more than a student reviewing it after the first 10 minutes.

Try not to get too worked up about Udemy's system of asking students to review your course very early on; those reviews do count less, but it at least gives Udemy some data about the initial impressions your course left on the student.

If you see a written one-star review from a student who completed your course, that is a true cause for concern. If there is any chance that review violates policies or is really a review of the platform, you need to flag it for review by Udemy, because it will do a lot of damage to your score. On the other hand, a one-star review left by a student who only watched your first lecture and didn't write any text is annoying, but it's something you can recover from more easily as you receive more reviews.

It's also important to realize that all reviews must pass through automated filters intended to block fraudulent reviews. If you give your mom or someone a free coupon for your course and ask her to leave a review on it, there's a good chance her review will never be posted if she didn't actually watch the content of your course first.

All too often, friends and family try to help by leaving a 5-star review on your course without even watching it. This looks a lot like a fake review that you may have paid for, and so Udemy might not allow it to go through. This "fake review filter" errs on the side of caution, since review fraud has become a real issue on the Udemy platform. As such, it may take even more effort for you to gather those all-important initial reviews on your new course.

Another source of ongoing maintenance is just keeping your course up-to-date. This is particularly an issue with technical courses. Technology changes so fast, that the way you teach something will probably be wrong in just a few months. New versions of software get released, technological advances are made, and little things get changed all the time that require you to update your course in order to keep it usable.

Listen to your Q&A, because that will probably be the first place where you hear about out-of-date content in your course. Review text might also start to mention this. Your students will let you know if your course is becoming outdated, and when that happens, you need to change your course accordingly.

If you're lucky, it's something small that just re-recording a portion of a single lecture can resolve. If you're not lucky, the topic you're covering has changed substantially all at once, and you need to re-record the entire course. In that case, you'll probably want to just release an entirely new course covering the new version of the technology at hand, and have coupons ready for all the students of your earlier course who demand an update.

There are steps you can take while developing content to minimize the risk of technology changes breaking your course. If you are teaching a software-related topic, make sure you instruct your students to install a specific version of all of the software in question.

Don't say "go to this website and download the latest version." Say "go to this website and download version 4.5 of the software, as that's what we're covering in this course." That will at least buy you some time when the next version comes out, since students taking your existing course won't be downloading software that doesn't work at all with it. You can update your course to work with the new version at your own pace, while students continue to learn with the earlier version of it.

For large, technical courses, keeping them up to date can become a significant effort. You really need to stay on top of it, because if you don't cover the latest technology, another instructor will - and take your future students away from you.

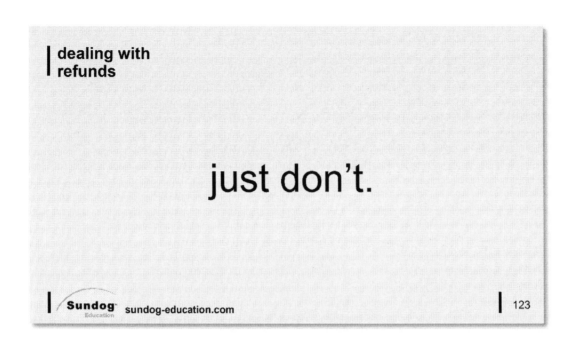

Many new instructors get very upset when a student gets a refund for their course.

There is nothing you can do about this, and you receive no actionable feedback from refunds. There is nothing to be gained by thinking about refunds. They are simply part of the game; a big part of how Udemy attracts new students is its no-risk, 30-day no-questions-asked refund policy. Yes, there are students who abuse this policy – however you're gaining more students than you are losing from refunds. Think of it from a student's perspective. Udemy has no accreditation, and no vetting of its instructors.

New students are really taking a leap of faith purchasing courses on this platform, and they need the security of that refund policy to give it a try. Seeing refunds of your course may be annoying, but on the whole it's a good thing for you.

The only thing you should think about with refunds is what your refund rate is. If it's more than say 5% of your revenue for a month that's been finalized, that's unusually high. It may be an indication that what you're promising on your course landing page and in your title, isn't what your course is actually delivering.

Make sure you're being honest with what your course delivers, and who it's for. Very high refund rates may be an indication of a real problem that you need to fix. Just remember, fixating on individual refunds from students is a waste of time, as there's nothing you can do about those individual cases.

Let Udemy find and police the students who are systematically abusing the system; that's their job, not yours.

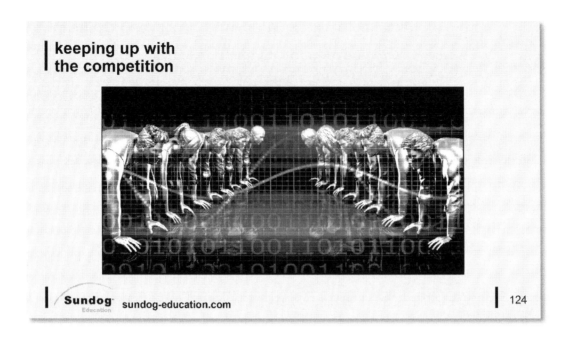

Once in awhile, especially if the sales of your course are declining, it's a good idea to check up on the competitive landscape.

Open up an incognito window in your browser, and search for your topic on Udemy. Are there new courses outranking you that you haven't seen before?

If so, why are they winning? Don't get angry about it; learn from it, and act on it. Did someone offer a course on the same topic, but with substantially more content? Perhaps it's time to add additional content to your course, as well. Is their A/V quality better than yours? Maybe it's time to re-record your course. Is their promo video professionally produced? Maybe it's time for you to do the same. Are they covering more recent information than you are? Maybe it's time for you to make some updates to your course.

Occasionally, you might catch someone who's cheating. Once I checked up on the competition for one of my courses, and found I was being outranked by a shorter course that had what seemed like an impossibly high review score. As I dug into their reviews, it started to become apparent that this competing instructor was purchasing 5-star reviews from some sort of review farm – many of them had similar text, many were in Russian, and many of them came from what looked like machine-generated user names. I flagged this to Udemy's policy team, and sure enough, within a few weeks that course was gone. It came back in a few months, but with the fake reviews no longer counting toward their score and with a much lower review score and search placement as a result.

Unfortunately, word has gotten out that there is money to be had on Udemy, and it's attracting some bad actors. It's worth checking if the instructors who are outranking you are playing on a level field. Courses that have a large number of reviews and an average of 4.8 or higher are suspect, and worth looking at critically.

Oh, and don't be a bad actor yourself. Remember, instructors like me are on the lookout for people buying fake reviews, and we will report you! I want you to succeed based on the merit of your work, not by cheating the system.

CHAPTER 11 – Licensing Your Course

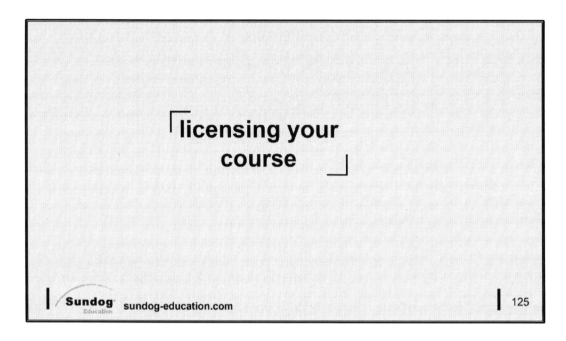

When you upload a course to Udemy, you are granting them a license to that course - though that license is non-exclusive. You're free to re-use that same content on other platforms, or even in different media, to reach an even wider audience. Let's talk about what's worked for me, and the platforms that I've learned to avoid.

First, I want to set expectations. Udemy is the metaphorical 800-pound-gorilla in the world of unaccredited online education. That is, if you can picture a friendly 800-pound gorilla – really, the people at Udemy are quite nice. But when it comes to platforms where you can just upload your own training videos without going through some extensive vetting process first, Udemy offers the largest opportunity to monetize your content. Other platforms I've used generate at most 3-5% of the revenue I generate on Udemy.

Set your expectations realistically. If you're not being successful on Udemy, you're probably not going to be more successful on some other platform. View other licensing opportunities as just a way to pull in a little bit of extra spending money, in a best-case scenario.

some other reputable platforms

- Skillshare
- Packt
- StackSkills / StackSocial
- CyberU
- O'Reilly
- LinkedIn Learning

Sundog Education sundog-education.com

The main alternative platform you should consider uploading your course to is Skillshare. Like Udemy, anyone can upload a course there, and usually you can just upload the same content you created for Udemy to Skillshare without issue.

There are a few important things about Skillshare that are different from Udemy, however. One is that they want you to provide a "final project" with your course. If you don't have one already, you'll have to think one up while you're creating your course there.

Another difference is that Skillshare is focused more on teaching creative skills, and not so much on technical skills. There is an audience for technical courses on Skillshare, but compared to Udemy it is very small.

Skillshare also does not pay you per enrollment; it pays you based on minutes watched. Skillshare students purchase a subscription plan, and not individual courses. So, your payment is based on how many minutes of your videos were watched by students on the Skillshare platform.

This subscription model also means that your course won't be at an advantage for being very long and comprehensive, as is the case on Udemy. It might be better to split up a large course on Udemy into several smaller courses on Skillshare.

Also, don't expect the same level of instructor support on Skillshare that you get used to Udemy. Skillshare has an "instructors to watch" program and unless they invite you into it, you won't get much in the way of personal support or advice as an instructor on SkillShare. Their user interface for creating courses is also pretty clunky and prone to errors, which can be frustrating.

In the end, it only takes a few hours to upload your Udemy course onto Skillshare, and there's really nothing to lose by doing so. Well, there is one consideration – Skillshare does not allow you to un-publish a course once you've uploaded it into their platform, so if you think you might have future plans of licensing your course exclusively to someone else, you might want to keep it off of SkillShare.

Skillshare is the only other large platform I've found where anyone can upload their course on their own. The remaining platforms I'm going to discuss will contact you if they want your content, not the other way around. As an instructor, you'll find there will be lots of platforms contacting you seeking to license your content, and it's important to know what you're getting yourself into when you do get that message.

Another somewhat large player in the online education space is Packt Publishing. Your experience with Packt will depend a lot on which group within Packt contacts you. Most often, they are looking for people to create exclusive, new courses for their platform, or for people to write books for them, also on an exclusive basis. I don't see any reason to create exclusive courses for a platform that is smaller than Udemy; why wouldn't you just make the same course, publish it on Udemy, and retain the rights to it yourself?

Writing a book for them may involve some small advance payment, but writing a book takes a lot of time and going back and forth with editors – that advance payment probably won't work out to be very good compensation for the time you put into it. I'd only consider authoring a book with Packt if you work primarily as a consultant, and the real value of writing a book is to use it to establish your authority and generate consulting leads.

Packt does on occasion, license courses on a non-exclusive basis. If they contact you asking to license a course you already made on Udemy non-exclusively, then by all means explore that deal.

I've found that the people who work in that part of the business are very good to work with, and often have some innovative programs such as creating books based on your video courses without any real involvement on your part. They can also get your course published on O'Reilly's Safari Online platform, which can open up a large audience for technical courses. I bring in a fair amount of extra cash by licensing my content to Packt on a non-exclusive basis, although it's still small compared to Udemy.

Some other book publishers, such as Manning, are also getting into this game. Although they are just starting out, I can vouch for them as good people to work with as well.

Another reputable player is StackSocial, or StackSkills. There's no real downside to doing business with these guys if they contact you. Their model is selling bundles of courses online on big media sites, so your revenue from them will be sporadic and tied to when they are promoting a bundle your course might be in. Their course creation UI was pretty buggy the last time I used it, however if you can work your way through it, it's basically free money. There's no expectation of supporting students on this platform, so it really is a case of uploading your course and forgetting about it.

I can also vouch for CyberU. The revenue they bring in for me is quite small, but it is revenue nevertheless. They do in fact pay you and are reputable people to work with.

If you're teaching technical topics, you might get contacted by O'Reilly publishing. This is a very prestigious brand in the field of technical education, and they are one of the few platforms where I have created some short courses on an exclusive basis. Getting in with O'Reilly can lead to further opportunities, such as writing or editing books and blog articles. Building a relationship with them is a great thing if you're given the opportunity.

Finally, there's LinkedIn Learning, formerly known as Lynda. You can apply to be an instructor with them on their website, which involves creating exclusive content for them – although instructors I've talked to report that these courses can be just as lucrative as courses on Udemy, so that is something worth considering. On rare occasions, they might reach out seeking to license your existing courses on a non-exclusive basis. However, they have very high technical standards and guidelines that your course must adhere to. If your existing course doesn't fit their style, they won't be interested once they take a closer look.

However, LinkedIn Learning is a large player, and it's worth modifying your course to meet their requirements if that's what they need from you. LinkedIn Learning can be a way to double your Udemy revenue if you can get published with them as well – but they are very picky about who they work with.

If some other platform contacts you looking for your course videos, my advice is to start with the assumption that they are out to scam you. You might think you have nothing to lose by licensing your content to some new online education company you've never heard of before; however, you'll think differently once they have taken your content, never pay you for it, and your course suddenly starts appearing on pirate sites. That has really happened to me, so please, learn from my mistakes.

The first thing to do when approached by a new company is to look at their website. Does it have things a real company would have, such as contact information with a real address, within a country where you can enforce a legal agreement? How established do they seem?

If they're just starting out, odds are you're not going to make any money with them, and you're risking just having your content stolen by working with them.

I don't want to name names, but I was even fooled into doing business with a startup who was using the name of a much larger brand, although their connection to that brand was tangential at best. I thought I was working with a large company, but in fact, it turned out to be just another startup that never paid me a dime for my content.

There are a few other reputable companies I haven't talked about, such as Udacity and Coursera. They tend to rely on real university professors to make their content, so unless you're a professor, you're not likely to be contacted by them.

Be aware that Udemy is working very hard behind the scenes to expand into more countries, and localize courses into other languages. If a startup from China contacts you promising to open up the Chinese market to you – you're probably better off waiting for Udemy to do that for you, instead. Especially if that Chinese company wants exclusive rights to your course in China. NEVER give away exclusive rights, in any territory, to a course you are publishing on Udemy. It's not the case that you have nothing to lose by working with a small online education startup you've never worked with before. You are risking having someone else sell the content you created as your own, and never paying you for it. You're also risking the legal expenses of reviewing whatever agreement they want you to sign. They do have a written agreement for you, right? If not, that's a sure sign that you're not dealing with a real company.

If you're going to be signing deals with other publishers for your online courses, do the responsible thing and find a business lawyer who can help you understand the terms of the agreements you're going to sign. They can alert you to potential problems, such as exclusivity terms, loopholes that allow them to not pay you, and making sure you have a way to back out of the deal if things go South. If you're not sure that a deal will cover the legal expenses of reviewing their agreement, then the deal probably isn't big enough for you to be wasting your time with it in the first place.

A contract review will cost at least a few hundred dollars. It's money well spent, just keep that in mind when you're deciding which deals to explore in more depth.

CHAPTER 12 – Udemy Full-Time

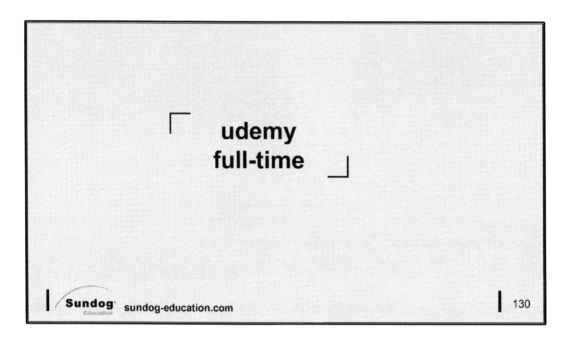

Too many people dive into Udemy expecting it to start paying their bills right away, and to take the place of a traditional job. Those people usually end up very frustrated when their Udemy income doesn't make that immediately possible. It is possible to make Udemy your full-time job, and in a responsible manner that doesn't put your livelihood on the line in the process.

Let's talk about making a living on Udemy, how to make that happen, and what the lifestyle really looks like.

Some people view Udemy as an easy path to freedom.

All you have to do is throw together a course in a month or so, then you can just kick back on the beach answering Q&A once in awhile as the money just flows in, right?

Sorry, wrong. Udemy is not a get-rich-quick thing, nor is it really passive income. If you plan to make online education your primary source of income, it's going to require sustained hard work from you.

Maintaining income from online courses requires constantly creating new courses. Your older course will make less and less money over time, and you need to keep ahead of that trend by always creating new courses to take their place – and keeping those older courses updated for as long as you can.

You're always looking for new ways to promote and market your courses, exploring new ways to license and publish them, and supporting your growing student base on top of all that. A typical day for me starts at around 6 AM, and ends at around 6 PM.

As we've talked about, becoming successful enough on Udemy for it to pay your bills is no easy task to begin with. Only perhaps the top 5% of Udemy instructors are able to do it full-time, so your odds of being able to quit your day job for Udemy are slim. That's just how it goes.

The things I've taught you in this guide will increase your odds, but a lot of it still comes down to your unique talents and skills, and how well they resonate with Udemy's students.

Becoming a full-time Udemy instructor is still a goal worth pursuing, however. Although you'll still be working hard, you'll be working with far fewer frustrations on a daily basis. Life is so much better when you don't have to deal with a daily commute or office politics.

Being your own boss means you never have to ask for permission if you want to live life a little. Want to take a quick little vacation somewhere, or even work abroad for months at a time? Nobody's going to stop you, and as a Udemy instructor, you can work from anywhere as long as you bring along the equipment you need.

Depending on your financial needs, maybe you don't have to work as hard as I do. The truth is, I could probably work half as much as I do if I didn't have a family of four to support. If it's just you, life as an online instructor could be a very liberating thing.

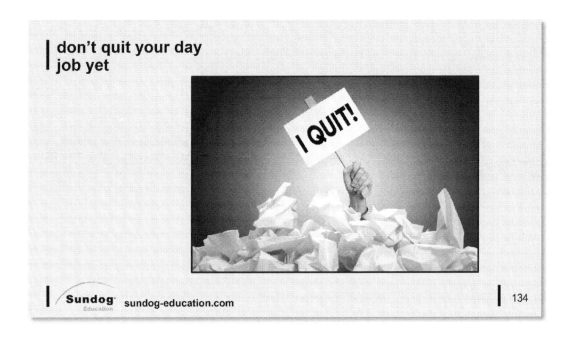

How to responsibly build up an online business and transition to it from a full-time corporate job is the subject of an entire book I once wrote.

To summarize the main point – don't just quit your day job, or whatever is currently providing your income, until you are sure that Udemy can replace that income – in addition to all the extra expenses you will incur once you are self-employed.

You need to start off treating Udemy as a "side hustle." When you get home from work, or on the weekends, chip away at creating your online courses. It will take longer when you're doing it in your spare time, but as long as you maintain a steady, disciplined effort, your course will eventually be ready to publish.

Then you can see how much revenue that course really brings in, and how it compares to your current source of revenue. Odds are you won't reach that level of success with a single course, so you're going to have to do it again, and maybe even again, all in your spare time. We're talking about a lot of extra work on top of the demands of your primary job; achieving this isn't easy. After publishing two or three courses, you should have a pretty good indication of what you're worth on the Udemy platform. If it's enough to pay the bills, great! You can consider taking the plunge. If not, well, you've got some extra income coming in that you didn't have before, and that's not so bad either, right?

Even if you do achieve substantial success with Udemy on the side, you need to remember this isn't a salaried job. Your income will vary, sometimes by a lot, from month to month. There will be good months, bad months, and maybe some trends you don't want to see over time.

So, you shouldn't quit your day job until you have saved up enough to at least survive long enough to find another job, should your Udemy revenue suddenly dry up. You never know what might happen; Udemy could decide to ban you from the platform, or even shut down itself. You have to be ready in case something like that comes to pass, by having enough financial reserves to pay your bills and put food on the table while you try to find a new job or source of income.

Try to start adding to your rainy-day fund as soon as possible. A general rule of thumb is to not quit your day job until you have at least 3 months' worth of savings, and Udemy has been generating enough revenue for you to live on for at least 3 months consecutively. Until that happens, just keep working on your courses on the side, in your spare time – but your main focus should still be your primary source of revenue, whatever that is.

Also, be careful when you're doing a "side hustle" such as this. It's up to you to make sure that the course you're making doesn't violate any employment, non-compete, or confidentiality agreements you may have with your current employer. If they do, the course you're making might get you fired before you're ready to do this full time. Never, ever work on your course while you're at your day job in any way, shape, or form. Using your company's time or equipment to create your course is another thing that can get you fired. You certainly don't want that!

When you're figuring out whether you've saved up enough to cover 3 months of living expenses, you also have to factor in that working for yourself can involve some significant expenses you didn't have before. You might think that all the money you'll save from not commuting will mean you can get by on less money, but in fact the opposite is true. Especially in the United States, being self-employed is a very expensive proposition.

I live in the US, so I can only speak to the expenses that exist here. If you live someplace else, you'll want to research what the real costs of being self-employed are in your own country.

The United States has what is called "self-employment tax." When you work for a company, that company pays for half of your Medicare and Social Security taxes. When you are self-employed, you are responsible for the full amount of those taxes.

How much that amounts to depends on how much money you're making, but for me I end up paying around a thousand dollars every month toward self-employment tax.

You also will not have an employer who is withholding your federal, state, and local taxes for you before you even see that money in your paycheck. If you're self-employed, you need to file estimated taxes every quarter, which means setting aside 20-30% of your earnings from Udemy and paying that to the IRS every three months. Whatever money you're making from Udemy, make sure you're taking taxes into account before you figure out if it's enough to live off of. If you don't pay your own estimated taxes, you could find yourself with a massive tax bill in April that you cannot pay – and you really don't want to be in that sort of situation with the IRS.

Even worse is health insurance. Since you can no longer get a group plan from your employer, where your employer was probably covering some of the cost, you have to purchase your own health insurance for you and your family. Individual plans are very expensive.

I pay over $2,300 every month to insure my family of four, and that plan has a $16,000 deductible I have to meet before it pays a penny. Factor in your increased insurance costs before you figure out how much money you'll need to survive every month on your own. If you live in a country with national health care, be very thankful for that.

If you become self-employed, you'll have to hire a lawyer to make sure you have set up your business properly, and to have someone on hand for any contracts you might need to have reviewed. Lawyers aren't cheap, so set up an initial consultation with a local lawyer who specializes in small businesses, and find out what sort of expenses you're looking at there.

As a self-employed person, your taxes will become much more complicated as well, and your risk of being audited increase too. You are going to need a good accountant who specializes in small businesses. Sometimes an accountant might recommend different corporate structures; for example, Sundog Education is actually set up as a Limited Liability Company that is treated as an S-Corporation for tax purposes, which reduces my self-employment tax a little bit. Doing that requires a lot of complicated paperwork and monthly and quarterly filings, as well as that need to file both corporate and individual taxes every year. It's not something you should even try to do on your own, unless you're an accountant yourself.

Depending on the corporate structure your lawyer and accountant recommends, you may also need business licenses at the state, county, and even local city level. These are generally annual expenses that aren't much in the grand scheme of things, but they are expenses nonetheless that you must account for.

Again, these are just the costs of self-employment in the United States. Other countries may be very different, and there may be additional expenses within different states within the United States. You'll need to consult with a lawyer and with an accountant to get a handle on what you're facing where you live.

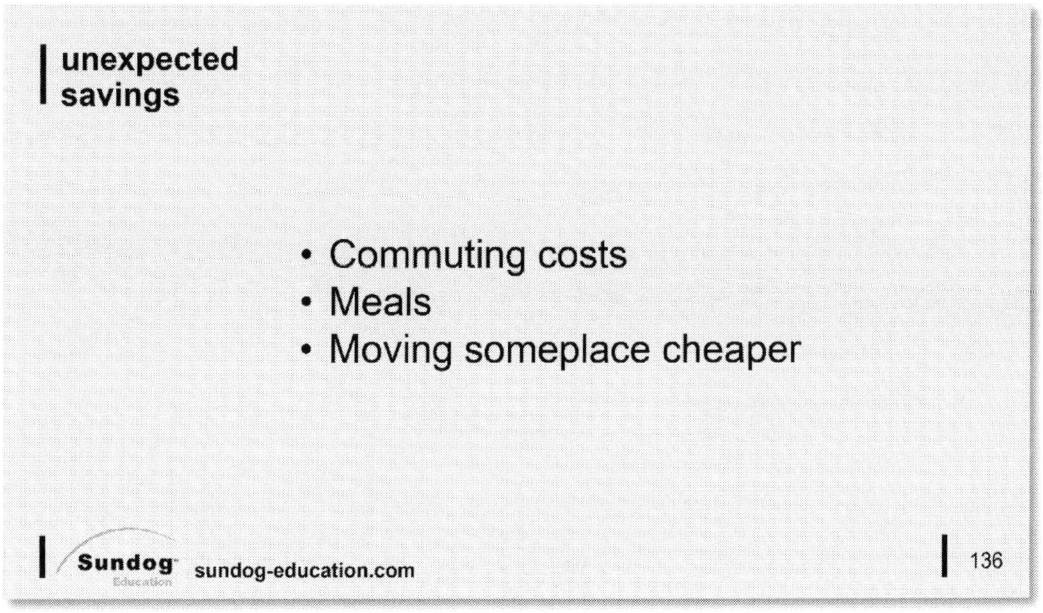

unexpected
savings
• Commuting costs
• Meals
• Moving someplace cheaper
Sundog
sundog-education.com
136

Working for yourself as an online instructor isn't all downside, though. There are also some ways in which you can save money, compared to working in an office for someone else.

If you work at home, then you can reduce your commuting costs significantly. Maybe you don't need that second car in your family any longer, or the insurance for it. You'll use a lot less gas, pay fewer tolls, pay less for parking, and spend less on vehicle maintenance too. Or maybe you can give up your expensive bus or train pass. For some people, this can really add up.

I'll bet you eat out more than you think at your corporate job. All those lunches at the cafeteria or local restaurants can really add up. When you work at home, you'll eat out of your fridge more often than not, and this can save money as well.

One of the biggest opportunities is taking advantage of the fact that you no longer need to live near your job. Maybe you can move someplace cheaper, and spend substantially less on housing, taxes, and your overall cost of living. I moved from Seattle to Orlando, where homes cost roughly one third of what they do in Seattle. There's also no state income tax here – and as an extra bonus, the weather's a lot nicer too. This can be huge; for what you'd pay to live in an apartment in San Francisco, you can live like a prince in a place like Florida – or live more modestly, and save a huge amount of money.

You need to be very sure that Udemy is going to be a *safe and sustainable* source of income in the long term before you move away from a big city, however. The reason you pay so much to live in a city is because cities are where the high-paying jobs are. If you move out into the countryside to save money, you might have to move back to the city if you need to go back to a corporate job. Don't move someplace cheaper until you have enough saved to cover both the cost of that move, and the cost of moving back should the need arise.

I hope I've drilled home the fact that becoming a full-time Udemy instructor is not something you should undertake lightly. Becoming successfully self-employed involves a lot of hard work, especially at first – and a lot of confusing, intimidating legal and accounting problems that you need to work through.

It's also scary when you walk out the door of the employer who's been giving you a steady paycheck, knowing that nobody is going to provide for you other than yourself now. It took at least a year before I wasn't living in fear of destitution after venturing out on my own.

It's worth repeating that not everyone can do it. Very few instructors reach the level of success where they can rely on Udemy income alone.

You need to prove to yourself that you can make it work before you quit your day job. Perhaps you need other sources of self-employment income to supplement it, such as doing contract work or live training.

If you can make it work, and do it responsibly, it's definitely worth it. It's hard for people to understand the freedom that comes with not working for someone else, and truly being able to do what you want, when you want to do it.

There's just no way to communicate what that feels like, and all the stress that disappears once you achieve that. Trust me, it's a goal worth striving for.

I hope the material in here has increased your odds of achieving it!

CHAPTER 13 – Wrapping Up

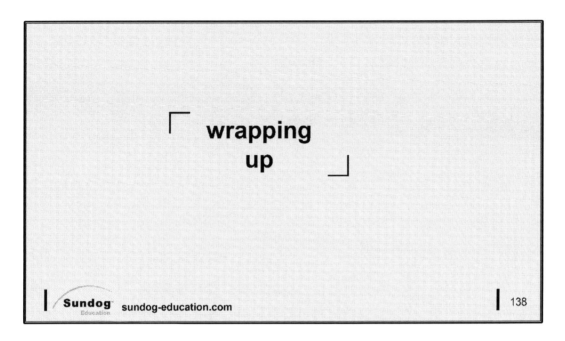

Congratulations, you made it to the end! At this point, I've told you everything I've learned throughout my 3-year, million-dollar journey as a Udemy instructor. You are now armed with all of the knowledge I had to learn the hard way, and you have all of the tools for success that I can give you. The rest is up to you! You need to apply what you've learned, work hard, and win the affection of your students - and never let up on your effort.

Udemy is a very competitive marketplace, and if you're not working hard at being successful in your category and maintaining that success, somebody else will. With these best practices in hand, your odds for success will be a lot better.

Now go make that next bestselling course!
See you in the marketplace!

NOTES

Printed in France by Amazon
Brétigny-sur-Orge, FR

14819928R00161